MANAGING MULTICULTURALISM IN THE CLASSROOM

(Dissertation)
Copyright © 2016 Arthur Boyer

i

Dr. Arthur Boyer, BSCJ, MPA, EdD

ISBN-13: 978-0692504109

ABSTRACT

This phenomenological study involved an examination of multiculturalism in classrooms and multicultural leadership. Ten transcultural college professors shared their daily lived experiences pertaining to their perceptions of multiculturalism in classrooms and multicultural leadership. The research encompassed a triangulation of individual interviews, a focus group, and the researcher's reflective journal. Findings revealed the increasing focus on multiculturalism in classrooms and accentuated its impact in the viability and vitality of the diverse American society. The researcher built the case for multiculturalism in diverse classrooms and multicultural leadership.

ACKNOWLEDGMENTS

First and foremost, I thank God for his blessings that have made me who I am today. Many other people to whom I am indebted played significant roles in the achievement of this academic milestone. This is my ultimate opportunity to thank them.

I thank my doctoral committee members, Gordana Pesakovic, PhD, and Patsy A. Kasen, DMgt, for having accepted to be my advisors. They led the journey with expertise, charisma, and wisdom. They taught me with their hearts, guided me to the highest standards, and ensured the successful completion of this journey.

I am indebted to Dr. Jeannette Brock, former President of Hodges University, and Leisha Cali, MA, Director of the ESL Department. I am also grateful to: Frank Perez-Mas, Jesus Hernandez, MD, Dr. Katherine N. Callard, Nancy Cheser, Stanislava Makhlouf, Dr. Denise Handapangoda, Lobar Araslanova, Andrew Holloway, Stephanie Swank, and Renee Newell. They always conveyed the great spirit of adventure with regard to education.

I thank Dr. Pender Noriega and Dr. Jackreece Telemate for their inspiring support. Their advice and feedback always brought some fresh air, better perspectives, and more desire for success. In addition, I thank Dr. Susan Ogletree and Professor Helene Cusack.

I extend my deepest gratitude to Professor Marie Jean Baptiste, MEdL, and Myrka Charles, RN. That was a journey between the best and the worst weathers. I thank you for your loving support, your constant encouraging words, your time, and your academic contribution.

Many other people contributed to the achievement of this project. Their multicultural voices stamped the significance of this research. I am grateful to Esther Moreno, M. You will always mean a lot to me. Your contribution was greatly appreciated. In addition, I thank Marie Guirlene Beldor, who could not wait to see the end of that study. I thank you Mrs. Jones. My cousin, Jean Robert Michel, played the academic inquisitor role of this project. He hired himself, and he did an excellent job. I also want to acknowledge my boy, Clifford Exalin.

This academic milestone is the tangible symbol of a lifetime of the utmost sacrifices, dedications, and commitments that Rev. Pastor, Emmanuel Boyer and Emita Zeme, my parents, have made toward my life. Father, this degree reflects the love, the values, and the powers you have instilled in me over the years, for which I am forever indebted to you. In addition, I want to acknowledge my brothers and sisters: Abed, Samuel, David, Bodelaire, Bodalie, Bodna, and Bodeline.

Arthur Boyer H., my son, played a major role in the achievement of this mission. He gave me the imperative reason to begin and accomplish it. He wanted to know why I was always busy reading and typing. Despite his young age, he never stopped supporting, encouraging, and believing in me. He was always ready to compromise all the quality time we were to have together, as father and son. I am very indebted to you, my son. This is done for you. I love you.

TABLE OF CONTENTS

Page

TABLE OF TABLES ix

CHAPTER ONE: INTRODUCTION 1
Problem Background 3
Purpose of the Study 4
Research Question.. 5
Definition of Key Terms 5
Significance of the Study 7

CHAPTER TWO: LITERATURE REVIEW................. 8
Openness to Multiculturalism................................ 9
Dimensions of Multicultural Conflicts 11
Managing Multicultural Conflict Dimensions................ 17
Implementing Multicultural Leadership 20
Building and Developing Multicultural Team Members
....24
Transformational Leadership Characteristics 27
Developing Affirming Multiculturalism 30
Teaching in Multicultural Classrooms 34
Empowering Educators to Lead Their Classrooms 39

CHAPTER THREE: METHODOLOGY 45
Research Design... 46
Research Question... 46
Research Participants 46
Research Instrumentation...................................... 48
Rigor and Validity 53
Methodological Assumptions 55
Methodological Limitations 55
Data Analysis... 56

CHAPTER FOUR: RESULTS 58
Individual and Focus Group Responses 59
CHAPTER FIVE: DISCUSSION, CONCLUSIONS,
AND RECOMMENDATIONS 108
Summary of the Study 109
Summary of Study Purpose 112
Research Design 112
Discussion of Results 113
Major Research Findings 114
Study Implications 116
Implications for Educational Institution 117
Implications for Organizations 118
Recommendations for Future Research 119
Generalizability and Limitations 122
Conclusion 124

REFERENCES 126

TABLE OF TABLES

Table		Page
1.	Participant Demographics	48
2.	Question 1 Emergent Themes	66
3.	Question 2 Emergent Theme	73
4.	Question 3 Emergent Theme	79
5.	Question 4 Emergent Theme	84
6.	Question 5 Emergent Theme	88
7.	Question 6 Emergent Theme	93
8.	Question 7 Emergent Theme	97
9.	Question 8 Emergent Theme	103
10.	Question 9 Emergent Theme	107

CHAPTER ONE

INTRODUCTION

The U.S. population is becoming more diverse, as the number of individuals in minority groups continues to increase. In 2006, the U.S. population comprised 81% Whites, 12.8% Blacks, 4.4% Asians, and 14.8% Hispanics (U.S. Census Bureau, 2008). The U.S. population will rise to 438 million in 2050, from 296 million in 2005, and 82% of the increase will be due to immigrants arriving from 2005 to 2050 and their U.S.-born descendants (Pew Research Center, 2014). It is projected that by the year 2050, 50% of the U.S. population will be racially and ethnically diverse (U.S. Census Bureau, 2008).

It is predicted that by the year 2050, one in two Americans will not be of Caucasian or European origin (U.S. Census Bureau, 2008). The immigrant population and their descendants will account for 96 million more over the next four decades (U.S. Census Bureau, 2008). It has been projected that by the year 2060, the percentage of the White population will decrease to 43% while the percentage of other groups will continue to increase (Pew Research Center, 2014). Trends indicate the following increases within other groups: African Americans up to 13%, Asians up to 8%, Hispanic up to 31%, and all other races to 6% (Pew Research Center, 2014).

Changes within the population will continue to play out in the development of the American society, the national economy, the workforce, and the education systems. For instance, in 2040, community college enrollment will reflect 57% Latino, about 25% Anglo, 10.2% Asian, and 8.1% Black students. On the other hand, public universities will count 44% Latino, 32% Anglo, 15% Asians, and 8.1% Blacks (Murdock, 2006).

In preparing students to succeed in the American workforce, school leaders are to develop an educational environment that prioritizes diversity. The personal, professional, and educational benefits of diversity are significant to the future of the American society (U.S. Department of Education, 2013). Students need the knowledge, skills, and abilities to effectively navigate their pluralistic environments. There must be resources, policies, and practices that embolden affirming diversity, quality teaching and learning, and sustainable success (Adam, 2010; Alston-Mills, 2011).

Problem Background

In a diverse school setting, leaders, educators, students, and classrooms represent a broad range of different ethnic, racial, cultural, professional, and educational background. These differences can pose constant and significant challenges (Alston-Mills, 2011; Barnhardt, 2014; Burdett & Crossman, 2012). Leaders and faculty members need to acknowledge, embrace, and openly address differences to be able to transform them into successful pedagogical tools by adding them to the curriculum and their leadership practices (Alston-Mills, 2011; Barnhardt, 2014).

A body of diverse faculty members can offer a fully-balanced viewpoint and picture of diversity and a dynamic teaching and learning environment that models the benefits of diversity, which can make it easier for students to transcend diversity boundaries (Alston-Mills, 2011; Burdett & Crossman, 2012). Faculty members bring with them their pools of knowledge, experiences, ideas, and professional and other diversity characteristics to work (Barnhardt, 2014; Wolfson, Kraiger, & Finkelstein, 2011). They can shape or influence the behaviors, expectations, visions, and educational goals of their students (DeSimone & Werner, 2012; Mello, 2011). However, leaders have to pave the way to a dynamic and diverse working and learning environment (Burdett & Crossman, 2012; DeSimone & Werner, 2012).

The cultural upbringing of educators influence many aspects of their lives, including their attitudes, perceptions, behaviors, motivation, beliefs, contributions, and so forth (DeSimone & Werner, 2012; Ford, 2005; Mello, 2011; Rice, 2005; Stahl, Maznevski, Voigt, & Jonsen, 2010). Their differences are to be acknowledged and well-managed because they can also significantly impact organizational operations and outcomes (Daft, 2008). Successes in diverse education institutions largely entails the invaluable academic experiences and cultural competence of the educators to value, accept, and embrace cultural differences among themselves, their students, and their daily lived experiences in their work environment (DeSimone & Werner, 2012; Igwebuike, 2006, Stahl et al., 2010).

Purpose of the Study

In this qualitative phenomenological study, the researcher explored the lived experiences of a diverse group of educators in their natural work setting and leadership practices within their institution. Professors can join their institution as culturally polar opposites and with a set of different expectations about themselves, their leaders, their co-workers, and their students (Dyer, Dyer, & Dyer, 2007). However, their daily lived experiences related to challenges and advantages working in a multicultural environment can make major differences on how they perceive their similarities and differences, their co-workers and their students, their work environment cultures, and their commitment to their institution (Daft, 2008; DeSimone & Werner, 2012; Igwebuike, 2006; Stahl et al., 2010). The researcher adopted the constructivist worldview and explored the phenomenon through the transcendental phenomenology approach. In using the transcendental phenomenology approach, the researcher cautiously conducted the study beyond all prejudgments (Creswell, 2009; Moustakas, 1994).

Research Question

What are the lived experiences of a diverse group of educators in their multicultural classrooms and the leadership practices developed within their institution?

Definition of Key Terms

Affirming diversity. Refers to the process of developing a culturally responsive environment (Nieto & Bode, 2012). In a culturally responsive setting, people of all diversity dimensions or background work proactively and assertively to make everyone feel acknowledged, fit, valued, and appreciated beyond all differences and similarities (Ford, 2005; Nieto & Bode, 2012; Schim et al., 2006).

Cultural competence. The process of the acknowledgement, integration, and transformation of knowledge of cultural similarities and differences about others (Capell, Dean, & Veenstra, 2008; Giger et al., 2007). Cultural competence entails awareness, attitudes, and behaviors that an individual can develop to respond respectfully and effectively to others of all diversity dimensions (Dudas, 2012; Purnell, 2005). Developing cultural competence is an invaluable journey to recognize, accept, embrace, and value the worth of self and others (Schim, Doorenbos, & Borse, 2006). Culturally competent individuals emphasize awareness, openness, and sensitivity toward others in order to adapt to their needs (Purnell, 2005; Schim et al., 2006).

Culture. A "shared learned behavior and meanings that are socially transferred in various life-activity settings for purposes of individual and collective adjustment adaptation" (Marsella, 2009, p. 122). Culture includes attitudes, axioms, perceptions, personhood, beliefs, consciousness, and values (Marsella, 2009; Rice, 2005; Stahl et al., 2010). It is about learning, developing, and sharing values (Chatman & Cha, 2003; Stahl et al., 2010). Each culture is unique, and people identify themselves with their cultural upbringing (Stahl et al., 2010).

Diversity. The existence of differences or the otherness among members within an environment (Jackson, May, & Whitney, 1995). The concept of diversity entails human characteristics and social attributes that cause individuals or groups to differ from others. The dimensions of diversity can be divided into two main categories: primary and secondary dimensions (Chatman & Cha, 2003; Rice, 2005). The primary dimension of diversity includes inborn human differences or human attributes, such as country of origin, ancestry, ethnicity, race, gender, age, religion, and sexual orientation (Dudas, 2012). An individual is always identified with these diversity attributes for they will always impact his or her life and will never change (Rice, 2005). The secondary dimension of diversity includes educational background, social-economic status, personal values, professional experiences, and religious beliefs. These diversity characteristics can be controlled and changed over the years (Jackson et al., 1995). Attributes from both sets of dimensions of diversity define an individual's self-portrait to self and others (Dudas, 2012; Rice, 2005).

Significance of the Study

American educational institutions are becoming increasingly diverse (National Center for Education Statistics, 2008). This study of the lived experiences of educators in a cross-cultural environment and the quality of their leader's leadership practices was of a timely significance for many reasons. Educational environments need culturally competent faculty members with the capacity to offer vehicles to prepare students academically as they help those students expand their knowledge and experiences and develop skills to interact and work across cultural differences (Barnhardt, 2014; Nieto & Bode, 2012). The study adds to the literature surrounding a multicultural education environment and multicultural leadership, and may be of interest to researchers, academicians, school leaders, and educators in multicultural environments.

CHAPTER TWO

LITERATURE REVIEW

Openness to Multiculturalism

Consistent demographic changes in the United States have led to the need for more diverse institutions (Barnhardt, 2014). Changes in structures, cultures, and programs are necessary to support and ensure the development of an increasingly diverse staff, faculty, and student body (Kitagawa & Oba, 2010). Those changes will attract and retain employees and students and maintain a more competitive environment (Lauring & Selmer, 2012; Visagie, Linde, & Havenga, 2011). In other words, if well-implemented, these changes will not only provide students with valuable and competitive educational experiences and knowledge, they will help with social and economic development (Ostergaard, Timmermans, & Kristinsson, 2011; Wolfson et al., 2011).

Leaders of multicultural institutions should play the predominant change agent role in helping members of their environment become aware of, accept, embrace, and value others, their differences, their cultures, their environmental norms, their beliefs, and their knowledge while developing well-strengthened multicultural working and lifelong learning environments (Antelo, Prilipko, & Sheridan-Pereira, 2010; Barnhardt, 2014; Clark, 2011; Ostergaard et al., 2011). Each diversity component can bring new values, ideas, strengths, or organizational dysfunctions into a multicultural environment (Barnhardt, 2014; Dyer et al., 2007).

Openness to diversity creates a consistent and compelling need for both leaders and members to take a proactive stance to value and encourage cultural intelligence, cultural differences, and cultural sensibility. Leaders and followers need to acknowledge that each member of the organization matters and is different, even those who share some similarities; thus, despite all complexities, cultural differences have their richness. Multiculturalism, if appropriately-managed, can foster opportunities, creativities, and productivities (Kankanhalli, Tan, & Wei, 2006; Liua, Nautab, Spectorc, & Lid, 2008; Ostergaard et al., 2011; Shockley-Zalabak, 2009). First, leaders and their followers have to know their cultural background and how they influence their lives, their environments, and their relationship with others (Antelo et al., 2010; Dyer et al., 2007; Wolfson et al., 2011).

All cultural differences and similarities matter. Multicultural organizations can benefit from committed support and openness to diversity (Lauring & Selmer, 2012). Both leaders and followers need to develop an environment that encourages openness to diversity. They may be able to make effective use of the resources of dissimilar members of their organization. In developing a multicultural climate, leaders and members will more likely feel the need to openly interact with one another accepting, valuing and debating their differences, and sharing their knowledge (Antelo et al., 2010; Chen, Wang, & Chu, 2011; Lauring & Selmer, 2012).

To develop viable openness to diversity, leaders must have a tacit understanding of the value of diversity (Castaneda & Bateh, 2013) and be able to draw a strategic picture of its trends and potential consequences if left unaddressed and develop productive strategies to help employees embrace the urgency to seek common benefits (Lauring & Selmer, 2012; Visagie et al., 2011; Wolfson et al., 2011). Lauring and Selmer (2012) argued that "since internationalization seems only to be more widespread and more important in the years to come, the knowledge about issues related to openness to diversity in multicultural settings could be valuable" (p. 796).

Openness to diversity emphasizes acknowledgment, acceptance, and tolerance for different opinions, worldviews, beliefs, knowledge, experiences, and cultural norms (Lauring & Selmer, 2012). Cultural diversity opportunities and trends impact all multicultural team operations either directly or indirectly (Visagie et al., 2011). It is vital that multicultural leaders acknowledge their responsibility to value the cultural differences of their followers and understand how those differences are increasingly affecting employees' commitment, professional and personal behaviors, motivations, and expectations, as each affects the organization's operations and outcomes (Daft, 2008; Wolfson et al., 2011).

Dimensions of Multicultural Conflicts

Regardless of the level of cohesiveness among team members, ideas related to innovation, productivity, creativity, and ways in which to counter a serious competitor will eminently create conflict within team members because, in most cases, everyone will have a particular opinion on how to make things better (Rahim, 2011). As beneficial as multiculturalism can be for the growth of both multicultural organizations and their employees, it can also impede business operations, organizational values, and socialization among leaders and members because cultural diversity is both a source of conflict and survival (Marsella, 2009). Ignoring or mismanaging cultural values in a multicultural workplace can exacerbate multiple organizational disadvantages (Doyle & George, 2008). Any disadvantageous issue, whether minor or major, can undermine the efficiency of team members. Organizational leaders are compelled to mobilize cultural differences and turn them into resources (Doyle & George, 2008; Liua et al., 2008).

Business operations largely depend on a series of decisions with which team leaders and members have to agree on a daily basis. For instance, some decisions may be as simple as rewarding an employee, while others may be as complex as taking disciplinary action against one or more employees or having to make major and uncertain organizational changes. Even what may look like the simplest team decision may, somehow, directly or indirectly, affect major operations of a team or the personal lives of others (Liua et al., 2008).

Both task and relationship conflicts are eminent in a multicultural environment (Doyle & George, 2008; Marsella, 2009). The approaches used to complete tasks vary from culture to culture. Different access to resources, different notions of time, judgments of the need, the nature, and the value of the tasks, personal role, relationship among co-workers and rewards associated with the completion of the tasks, and even gender differences may come in to play when it comes to structuring and performing tasks (Liua et al., 2008; Marsella, 2009). For instance, studies have shown that contrary to European-Americans who primarily focus on task completion and let relationships build and develop as people work, individuals from Asian and Hispanic cultures value the need to build relationships at the beginning of team projects and then focus on task completion (Liua et al., 2008). Neither approach diminishes or adds more value to any of those cultural concepts; they are simply different. As different as team members may be, they need to develop and maintain a shared sense of purpose when structuring tasks such as setting their agendas focusing on tasks to be completed, selecting team members, and assigning clear and specific roles and responsibilities. Nevertheless, task structure and completion factors differ significantly across cultures (Daft, 2008; Shockley-Zalabak, 2009).

The quality of the relationships among leaders and members can reveal and profoundly impact organizational operations (Shockley-Zalabak, 2009). Multiple types of personal conflict styles have been studied. They imply both individual and organizational needs, interests, and goals. Shockley-Zalabak (2009) suggested the following conflict styles:

- *Avoidance.* Individuals preferring the avoidance style are unlikely to pursue their own goals and needs or to support relationships and the goals and needs of others during conflict.
- *Competition.* The individual who prefers competition approaches conflict by emphasizing personal goals and needs without considering the opinions or needs of others in the conflict.
- *Compromise.* Compromisers prefer to balance people concerns with task issues and often approach conflict with a give-and-take attitude that contributes to negotiation.
- *Accommodation.* People who want to be liked, have high affiliation needs, or genuinely are

concerned for the needs of others often prefer an accommodative approach to conflict.

- *Collaboration.* Individuals who prefer collaboration can behave collaboratively only when others assume a collaborative orientation and have enough task or goal information to solve the problem thoroughly (pp. 307-308).

Communication is a key factor in relationship conflicts (Shockley-Zalabak, 2009). Effective exchanges are vital in a multicultural environment (Castaneda & Bateh, 2013). Lunenburg (2010) made the case that "the better the leader-member exchange relationship between leader and follower, the higher the productivity, job satisfaction, motivation, and citizenship behavior of the follower" (p. 3). Exchanges are not always consistent because leaders usually have varying relationships with their followers (Castaneda & Bateh, 2013; Shockley-Zalabak, 2009).

In some cases, the level of responsibility, number of years with the organization, and roles can define the quality and level of the relationship or exchanges between a subordinate and a leader. Leaders and their followers can form high-quality exchanges that are based on trust and liking, or they can have low-quality social exchanges. Low-quality exchanges are usually based on lack of trust and do not extend beyond basic employment requirements. High-quality leader-member relationships can increase the level of latitude that leaders entrust to their followers (Castaneda & Bateh, 2013; Cheng, Wang, & Zhang, 2011).

Leader-member exchange follows three specific stages: the stranger stage, communication stage, and maturity stage (Cheng et al., 2011). The stranger stage reflects the leadership practices of the leader. In the second stage, leaders and followers start to develop two-way communication. Upon the quality of their communications, their relationship can expand. This leads to the maturity stage, which entails reciprocal trust, loyalty, and respect between leaders and followers. Leaders and followers can influence each other's roles within their organizations (Cheng et al., 2011; Lunenburg, 2010).

One major issue that can seriously impede member-member and leader-member exchanges is language dissimilarities within the organization (Cheng et al., 2011; Dyer et al., 2007). Lauring and Selmer (2012) documented: "In a multicultural organizational environment that is generally tolerant to the speaking of different languages, groups members will experience a higher level of trust and lower levels of conflict" (p. 797). The meanings of spoken, nonverbal, and written languages vary within and among cultures (Lee, Park, Lee, & Lee, 2007). People use words and phrases or add different meanings to words and phrases within their own and other cultures. On the other hand, nonverbal communications, such as facial expressions, other types of body movements, maintaining personal distance, tone of voice, sense of time, and other forms of nonverbal communication may also be sources of misunderstanding (Lee et al., 2007; Lunenburg, 2010; Madhlangobe & Gordon, 2012).

The way an individual uses words, phrases, and nonverbal expressions, their real meaning, and their interpretations by others can foster feelings and thoughts that can develop, sustain, or inhibit relationships. Just like any other diversity trends, language dissimilarities among employees and leaders can become a valuable organizational asset (Madhlangobe & Gordon, 2012). However, it takes leaders who can focus "on tangible qualities such as vision, shared values, and ideas in order to build relationships, give larger meaning to separate activities, and provide common ground to enlist followers in the change process" (Daft, 2008, p. 356; see also Madhlangobe & Gordon, 2012).

As costly as some organizational conflicts may be, some conflicts are a necessity for the organization. They can propel innovation, creativity, productivity, and sustainable success (Liua et al., 2008; Rahim, 2011). For instance, culture conflicts can be either constructive or destructive. Destructive conflicts can run for long periods and end in uncontrolled escalation cycles and animosity among members (Daft, 2008; Liua et al., 2008). In expressing some direct conflict behaviors, employees may be involved in hostile arguments or power struggles, make undermining comments, conduct retaliation, or falsely accuse each other (Marsella, 2009). Those behaviors can impede interactions between team members, organizational commitment, and production (Dyer et al., 2007; Shockley-Zalabak, 2009). Positive cultural conflicts, which leaders need to encourage, can impel common understanding, sensitivity, mutual respect, appreciation, trust, and collective interests (Marsella, 2009; Shockley-Zalabak, 2009).

Managing Multicultural Conflict Dimensions

Bennis (1994) stated: "Leaders learn by leading, and they learn best by leading in the face of obstacles" (p. 146). Sometimes, what may be perceived as the best conflict resolution approach by many may be overlooked by others because of personal past experiences, mistakes in judgment, lack of information, or just because they want to be different (Kankanhalli et al., 2006). Developing an effective conflict management approach is imperative. In some cases, as Clegg, Kornberger, and Rhodes (2007) noted, "the model of decision-making is described as a perfectly well-organized, rational logical process. Processes are defined, the relevant information is analyzed, possible solutions are generated, and the optional solution is decided upon and implemented" (p. 397). In other cases, even the most experienced leader may be challenged because each conflict is unique and there is no "one-size fits all" conflict management approach (Clegg et al., 2007; see also Daft, 2008; Maharaj, 2007).

In working with subordinates to develop strategies to manage multicultural conflict dimensions and diversity awareness, Joplin and Daus (1997) suggested that leaders may have to face the following six innovative change trends:

- *Change of power dynamics.* Appears to function smoothly; Latent, suppressed power struggles.
- *Diversity of opinions.* Explicit disrespect / visible disdain of minorities; minorities fail to voice their opinions due to expected sanctions.

- *Perceived lack of empathy.* Occasional eruptions between factions with primarily under the surface tensions; discounting of minority contributions.
- *Tokenism, real and perceived.* Resentful; often exaggerated expressions toward those with apparent diverse characteristics; attribute minority failures to stereotype category and success to chance / benevolence of the organization.
- *Participation.* Employees see participation as exercise in futility. Learned helplessness exhibited by employees.
- *Overcoming inertia.* Preceding issues a relative nonissue except when the minority voices their position on major issues (Joplin & Daus, 1997).

In managing organizational conflicts and developing effective organizational decision-making approaches, leaders have to be open-minded in collecting valuable information and avoid detrimental mistakes in judgment to avoid feelings of guilt, uncertainty, and self-recrimination. "While mistakes are to be avoided if possible, leaders who dwell on them only compound the problem. Feelings of guilt can be distracting and cause a loss of focus and an inability to deal with the next challenge" (Perkins, Holtman, Kessler, & McCarthy, 1942, p. 68).

Cheng et al. (2011) emphasized the following organizational decision-making approaches:

A two-stage decision-making process is widely used in management teams in China. In the first stage, which we have called the consensus discussion stage, the team leader allows team members to share and discuss their opinions without commenting on them (as in the consensus approach). In the second stage, which we have called the leader decision stage, the leader joins in the discussion and makes the final decision (as in the hierarchical distributed expertise approach). Because conflicts changed in this process we proposed that relationship conflict would be induced by, and positively correlated to task conflict in the consensus discussion stage. In the leader decision stage, relationship conflict would be reduced, while task conflict would facilitate decision performance. (p. 190)

Leaders have to put everything on the discussion table, collect all necessary information, conduct in-depth analysis of the issue, and involve the whole team to work toward a holistic decision-making process. A holistic approach will bring more ideas, reduce personal expectations and emotional weaknesses, and establish stronger personal interactions (Savory & Butterfield, 1999).

Team diversity can be beneficial in the decision-making process as it can bring more voices, more suggestions, and strengthen leaders' confidence (Daft, 2008; Zaccaro, Rittman, & Marks, 2001). "Diversity can contribute to a healthy level of conflict that leads to better decisions" (Daft, 2008, p. 300). "Effective teams are those that are able to maintain high levels of collective performance . . . high level performance requires that teams develop norms and operating procedures that promote individual and collective flexibility and adaptability" (Zaccaro et al., 2001, p. 457). As leaders seek inclusion in the decision-making process, they need to avoid practices that can force members to make faulty decisions in order to avoid peer pressure or being rebuked, which usually leads to more negative conflicts because it involves an illusion of invulnerability, stereotyped views of out-groups, self-censorship, and collective rationalization (Daft, 2008; Dyer et al., 2007; Shockley-Zalabak, 2009).

Implementing Multicultural Leadership

Leaders play the most fundamental role in developing a multicultural work environment. They must be able to successfully motivate and stimulate members to openly value themselves and their cultural background, securely transcend their self-expectations to acknowledge others, and work together to transform diversity trends into long-term benefits (Madhlangobe & Gordon, 2012). Leaders need to share their organizational vision with their followers, inspire them to embrace the vision, build common interests, goals, and values, and acknowledge and embrace similarities and differences (Daft, 2008; Wolfson et al., 2011).

Implementing change is not an easy task (Hansuvadha & Slater, 2012). Change facilitators must expect resentment and resistance because people identify themselves with their cultures. Thus, any attempt to change that perspective may be seen as cultural ignorance, personal disrespect (Daft, 2008). Change is a process with multifaceted developmental stages. With quality cultural intelligence, one can learn to acknowledge the need to develop the "ability to function comfortably in cross-cultural settings and to interact harmoniously with people from cultures that differ from their own" (Hansuvadha & Slater, 2012, p. 175). Instead of ignoring or trying to define for themselves cultural contexts, people's knowledge can help them more openly overcome their psychological and emotional strains to accept the unfamiliar, go beyond their assumptions, sense and value others' feelings, become better communicators, or even enrich their own cultures and knowledge just by learning a new language (Hansuvadha & Slater, 2012; Madhlangobe & Gordon, 2012).

Joplin and Daus (1997) found that, "As diversity is introduced into a workplace, leaders must take a more proactive stance toward their own involvement with employees as work practices and routines are reviewed and, if need be, revised" (p. 33). In implementing leadership practices that incorporate acknowledgement and acceptance of the richness of diversity within a multicultural environment, leaders can successfully model the way for their employees and others to do the same. Roper (2011) suggested a "multicultural supervisor is able to move with ease into and out of different cultural contexts, creating a history of culture-affirming as he or she goes" (p. 79).

The emotional intelligence of leaders is vital in the course of leadership practices (Mayer, Salovey, & Caruso, 2004). It allows leaders to accurately perceive, access, and generate their own and their followers' emotions, "so as to assist thought, to understand emotions and emotional knowledge, and to reflectively regulate emotions so as to promote emotional and intellectual growth" (Mayer et al., 2004, p. 197). Well-developed emotional intelligence can help build stronger and longer bonds between leaders and followers (Barbuto & Burback, 2006; Mayer et al., 2004). "Emotional bonds are implicit in transformational leadership behaviors. Leaders who respond empathetically to co-workers can improve organizational effectiveness" (Barbuto & Burback, 2006, p. 53; see also Bennis, 1944).

Leaders have a moral responsibility to develop, support, motivate, and care for their subordinates (Canfield-Davis, Tenuto, Jain, & McMurtry, 2011). Leaders have to offer and model the pathway toward innovative change. Leaders' behaviors, actions, broader range of skills, moral character, quality of their exchanges with their subordinates, and their dedication to the well-being of their subordinates are baseline requirements for success. Leadership approaches must envisage the vision, mission, values, culture, and core values of the team or organization, and moral standards of the leaders (Canfield-Davis et al., 2011; Joplin & Daus, 1997).

In emphasizing high moral standards, leaders can develop an environment of trust, loyalty, rightness, and fairness. "The function of morality . . . is to create altruism by making human beings to follow impersonal ends. Altruism, in turn, makes a harmonious community of endeavors for the collective interest possible" (Barmaki, 2008, p. 52). Bennis (1994) highlighted the following concepts that leaders can use to generate and sustain an environment of high moral standards:

- *Constancy.* Whatever surprises leaders themselves may face, they don't create any for the group.
- *Congruity.* Leaders walk their talk. In true leaders there is no gap between the theories they espouse and the life they practice.
- *Reliability.* Leaders are there when it counts; they are ready to support their co-workers in the moments that matter.
- *Integrity.* Leaders honor their commitment and promises. (p. 161)

These concepts can be used as yardsticks to lead. Kouzes and Posner (2008) contended that "leaders practice what they preach—they are serious about their duty to represent their values and standards to the rest of the world and to live up to them the best of their abilities" (p. 37). Effective leadership practices can significantly encourage followers "to demonstrate increased loyalty, confidence, and to have a stronger sense of emotional well-being" (Webb, 2007, p. 68).

Leaders are expected to seek the best interests of their subordinates and their environment (Daft, 2008; Dyer et al., 2007; Webb, 2007). Respect, honesty, loyalty, and impartiality of leaders toward their subordinates can make major differences in how those subordinates perceive their leaders, their co-workers, business operations, and the culture of their environment. The moral qualities of the leaders will always come in to play even when leaders and their followers have to face uncertain business choices, such as taking critical disciplinary actions or evaluating considerations for organizational rewards (Kidder, 1995).

Multicultural leaders need to show high moral standards in their customary leadership practices (Daft, 2008; McCoy, 2007).

All throughout their leadership operations, leaders must strive to show good moral practices. However, "One must be willing to lose, as good practice is not always supported by the enterprise" (McCoy, 2007, p. 80). Leaders need to consistently stay in touch with their guiding principles. Kidder (1995) suggested that "the claims of justice urge us to stick by our principles, hold the rules despite the pressure of the moment, and pursue fairness without attention to personalities or situations" (p. 138). Effective leadership actions involve the greatest good for the greatest number (Daft, 2008; Kidder, 1995).

Building and Developing a Multicultural Team

In their mission to meet the challenges related to continuing demographic changes, leaders of multicultural institutions need to develop a well-aligned and trained, coordinated, and cohesively committed team. Leaders need a team that can seek and gain all competitive advantages from cultural differences. It is critical that leaders know what drives their employees' choices in action, attitudes, commitment, behaviors, and contributions to their work environment. Maxwell (1995) stated, "Good coaches know what their people prefer, and they use that knowledge to attain the team's and the individual player's goals" (p. 149). Person-organization fit is a necessity as it is an important aspect of both employment and team development. Leaders need to know their employees and what they want.

Employees join organizations with needs that must be met, which can include both biological and psychological needs. They may also have high expectations that their values, ability, cultural differences, functional skills, and personal and professional goals will be acknowledged and appreciated. On the other hand, leaders have their own needs, values, interests, and expectations from their employees (Daft, 2008; Dyer et al., 2007).

It is very important that needs and expectations match (Daft, 2008). The needs, values, and interests of both individuals and organizations must be aligned and valued. Leaders and their employees must be able to establish that compatibility (Liu, Liu, & Hu, 2010). This process most likely begins during the job interview, which gives both leaders and potential employees the opportunity to emphasize and discuss their differences and find their fit or their compatibility. Perkins et al. (1942) suggested "a unified team is one in which every member understands the task to be done and feels a sense of deep personal responsibility for the success of the group's efforts" (p. 79).

In seeking to establish their fit, both leaders and followers must understand that their needs, values, interests, and expectations are subject to change at any time. Their characteristics must remain congruent; however, at times, they will need to compromise. For instance, all employees' needs will not be met; however, leaders need to know their employees' needs and expectations even when some of them do not directly or indirectly relate to the work environment (Dyer et al., 2007; Keung & Rockinson-Szapkiw, 2013; Maxwell, 1995).

Maxwell (1995) contended that, "Once a leader is genuinely interested in the well-being of those around him, the determination and drive of the people in that group are activated in a remarkable way" (p. 22). For instance, educators will face consistent challenges to make an invaluable connection between their cultural differences, perceptions, expectations, professional and personal needs, and goals. They have joined their institutions as culturally polar opposites and with a set of different expectations about themselves, their leaders, and their co-workers, but their daily lived experiences related to challenges and advantages can make major differences in how they perceive their differences, their work environment, their commitment, their contribution, and how they relate to one another (Daft, 2008; Keung & Rockinson-Szapkiw, 2013).

The better the person-organization fit the easier it is for leaders to more effectively manage their environment and motivate and develop their followers while meeting organizational goals. Effective leaders acknowledge the need to consistently enable their followers to share their ideas, use their unique skills and talents, and show their hearts (Daft, 2008; Maxwell, 1995; Prilipko, Antelo, & Henderson, 2011). Person-organization fit has a "strong positive effect on job satisfaction and a negative effect on turnover intention" (Liu et al., 2010, p. 623).

Acknowledging employees' functional skills, experiences, and cultural background is a means of increasing their "power, energy, and freedom of intentional choice in their diverse work environment" (Pedersen & Connerly, 2005, p. 7). "Multicultural awareness, knowledge, and skills increase a person's intentional and purposive decision-making ability by accounting for the many ways that culture influences different perceptions of the same solution" (Pedersen & Connerly, 2005, p. 7). If appropriately managed, cultural differences within the environment may bring different significant contributions for real and sustainable outcomes (Keung & Rockinson-Szapkiw, 2013).

Transformational Leadership Characteristics

The transformational leadership style can help school leaders facilitate change and transform their employees (Daft, 2008; Northouse, 2001). Transformational leaders can develop effective approaches and practices by assessing followers' expectations, needs, and motives to encourage them to want to change. Idealized influence, inspirational motivation, intellectual stimulation, and individual consideration define transformational leaders (Northouse, 2001). These components describe invaluable characteristics that transform leaders into role models, innovators, inspirers, encouragers, and coaches (Dyer et al., 2007; Northouse, 2001). Transformational leaders make continued efforts with unwavering commitment to be always visible, listening, doing the rounds, enthusing, and soothing their followers (Keung & Rockinson-Szapkiw, 2013; Prilipko et al., 2011; Northouse, 2001).

Idealized Influence
Transformational leaders are exemplary role models. They use their idealized influential powers or their charisma to earn the trust, respect, and hearts of

their followers while strengthening their team (Prilipko et al., 2011). They prioritize open leader-member relationships and add value to their followers' voices in organizational activities and decisions without pre-determined command or intimidation, which can foster vital qualities within the organization. As a result, followers identify themselves with the leader, embrace a deep sense of organizational mission and goals, and perform beyond expectations (Northouse, 2001).

Inspirational Motivation

Transformational leaders motivate their followers to meet organizational goals. They embrace needs, seek team spirit, support and ensure its utmost efficiency, and make change happen to reach personal and organizational goals and encompass contingent reward. Inspirational motivation enables followers to transcend their self-interests and meet their leaders' expectations, and leaders instill pride in them (Barbuto, 2005; Northouse, 2001; Yukl, 1998).

Intellectual Stimulation

In trying to facilitate change within their organizations, transformational leaders strongly support creativity and innovation, turn the work environment into a learning environment, and convert trends into opportunities. They consistently challenge themselves, their followers, and current organizational norms and cultures. Such leadership behaviors increase followers' commitment, interests, and involvement in organizational issues and encourage them to play leadership roles. Otherwise, the team may lack competency or members may lack the intellectual capacity to capitalize on their competencies to succeed (Barbuto, 2005; Dyer et al., 2007; Northouse, 2001). Transformational leaders stimulate the intellectual and mental capacity of their followers (Prilipko et al., 2011; Northouse, 2001).

Individual Consideration

Transformational leaders lead as organizational and individual coaches and advisors to help followers reach leaders' expectations. They personally know their followers (in some instance, their family members). They know their skills, their competencies, and even the level of their organizational commitment and satisfaction (Dyer et al., 2007). Such personal knowledge of their followers enables leaders to better influence their followers. Transformational leaders understand the vital importance of investing in the personal and professional development of their employees. Under this leadership dimension, leaders also show honest acknowledgment and give praise and rewards for personal and organizational achievements (Dyer et al., 2007; Northouse, 2001).

Transformational leadership approaches are not the only solution to developing a successful multicultural environment. Successful transformational leaders have the vital power to embrace their challenges as business opportunities and seek direction to explore possible routes. Even in uncertain situations, they make others follow them with commitment, trust, respect, and enthusiasm (Komives, 2010; Northouse, 2001).

Developing Affirming Multiculturalism

Continuous efforts to manage cultural diversity can make it easier to develop a more sustainable affirming diversity climate, which can foster mutual respect, commitment, and empowerment (Elems, 2011; Wolfson et al., 2011). In an environment that affirms cultural diversity, employees are more likely to openly listen, accept differences, and demonstrate attitudinal attachment to their organization and create sustainable relationships and exchanges with others (Elems, 2011). These components can improve the understanding of the nature and implications of cultural diversity, which can help members to acknowledge their cultural bias, their similarities, their priorities, and their common grounds (Doyle & George, 2008; Elems, 2011).

When developing an affirming diversity climate in a multicultural environment, Cox (1991, as cited in Wolfson et al., 2011), suggested the following six organizational conditions:

- *Pluralism*, which exists when organizational norms and values are influenced by both majority and minority group members.
- *Full structural integration*, which exists when members of all demographic groups are well-represented in all levels and job functions throughout the organization.
- *Full integration of the informal networks*, which exists when members of all demographic groups feel welcome in informal social gatherings.

- *Low cultural bias*, which exists when discrimination and prejudice throughout the organization are minimized or eliminated.
- *Minimal intergroup conflict*, which exists when there is minimal tension between members of different sociocultural groups.
- *Organizational identification*, which exists when employees identify with and are dedicated to their organization (Wolfson et al., 2011, p. 163).

As the environment becomes more multi-culturally affirming, people may develop a stronger sense of confidence and security to go beyond their cultural differences and become a unified team with a tacit knowledge of the roots of their differences, their challenges, their common interests, and their actions (Perkins et al., 1942, p. 79).

> When employees perceive that the organization . . . cultivates an affirming diversity climate, they . . . feel valued and fulfilled in their job, develop loyalty towards and attitudinal attachment to the organization, and experience improved interactions with co-workers. (Wolfson et al., 2011, p. 163)

Affirming diversity can facilitate sustainable positive climate perceptions (Wolfson et al., 2011). However, leaders first need to provide their members with a clear vision, support, encouragement, training, empowerment, constant feedback, and tangible resources for them to be able build a sustainable framework that emphasizes interdependency of cultures, team effectiveness, common values and opportunities, theoretical and personal skills, and transcendental goals (Wolfson et al., 2011).

The first four multicultural dimensions of Hofstede's (1991) dimensions—power distance, uncertainty avoidance, individualism versus collectivism, and masculinity versus femininity—offer transformational leaders invaluable leadership tools to facilitate their relationships with their followers and inspire their followers to follow them (Hofstede, 1991). These dimensions, as defined in the following sections, explain how Hofstede conceptualized culture in terms of meaning.

Power Distance

Hofstede (1991) found countries with low power distance and others with high power distance. The concept of power distance refers to the acceptance of the nature of human relations in terms of power and inequality in the exercise of authority, wealth, privilege, and social status within a society. In high power distance cultures, authority figures (e.g., community leaders, parents, teachers, and other superiors) are facts of life, and they emphasize decisions over their environments. Power is centralized, and followers have to express obedience because they expect an unequal distribution of power (Hofstede, 1991; Triandis, 2001). Hofstede (1991) concurred, stating power distance is "the extent to which less powerful members of institutions and organizations within a country expect and accept that is distributed unequally" (p. 28).

Uncertainty Avoidance

This concept focuses on societies that emphasize a certain degree of uncertainty and ambiguity among their people. Some unstructured and uncertain conditions, such as certain sudden changes within an environment, can foster either comfortable or uncomfortable feelings. People tend to respond to uncomfortable feelings through deviant or uncontrollable behaviors. The level of their uncertainty usually defines their reactions and the measures adopted by authorities to manage the situations (Hofstede, 1991).

Individualism versus Collectivism

These concepts define specific diction of countries, values, and cultures (Triandis, 2001). In individualist countries, individuals are considered the most important unit of their environment and are expected to take care of themselves and their immediate relatives, stand up for themselves and relatives, and strive for individual rights and personal achievement (Holmes, Sherman, & Williams-Green, 1997). On the other hand, in predominantly collectivist societies, individuals live as members of their groups, families, or organizations. Collectivists identify themselves with their groups and environments, express unquestioning loyalty to others, and holistically seek the greater good of all (Hofstede, 1991; Holmes et al., 1997; Triandis, 2001).

Masculinity versus Femininity

Cultures vary across masculinity versus femininity. As Hofstede (1991) found, some cultures differentiate gender roles in their environments and place different values on both men and women.

Cultures that place high values on men emphasize a preference for performance, assertiveness, achievement, wealth, and ambition. However, in more feminine societies there is a focus on social accommodations, concern for the weak, nurturing behaviors, quality of life, modesty, interpersonal relationships, and environmental awareness (Hofstede, 1991).

Teaching in Multicultural Classrooms

The need for school leaders to develop more diverse campuses has become a tacit national priority (Burdett & Crossman, 2012). For instance, by the year 2040, although the American Anglo community will become a minority group, it will still be the majority group in higher education at nearly 57% (Murdock, 2006). On the other hand, the Asian, African American, and Latino populations will remain almost the same with about 14% each (Murdock, 2006).

Culturally competent educators understand the need to use culturally sensitive approaches to ensure equitable prospects that incorporate the individual fulfillment, personal or professional development, and the academic success of all students regardless of their cultural background (Burdett & Crossman, 2012; Pedersen & Connerly, 2005). There is always a sense of urgency for school leaders and educators in multicultural settings to be culturally competent (Igwebuike, 2006). A lack of cultural competency can pose serious leadership dysfunctions for school leaders (Dudas, 2012; Pedersen & Connerly, 2005).

Cross-cultural intelligence enables educators to be aware of and sensitive to their own cultural background, values, attitudes, beliefs, and functional skills while they embrace their followers' differences. As Pedersen and Connerly (2005) contended, "The more leaders know about cultural influences, the better able they will be to direct the organization by understanding the behaviors of both their own employees and others outside the organization" (p. 16). In modeling expected behaviors, leaders may be able to take their followers (educators) beyond their self-interests, ethnocentric feelings, fear of accepting differences and the unfamiliar (Kouzes & Posner, 2008). Despite the complexity of cultures, employees can learn to securely embrace cultural differences, appreciate, and celebrate them in all their values, their richness, and their complexity (Daft, 2008).

Educators with strong cultural intelligence are likely to transform cultural differences within their environment into pedagogical and social opportunities for the benefit of their students (Barnhardt, 2014). Instead of ignoring their students' differences, they can help them develop an awareness of their own cultures and those of others. It is invaluable for both school leaders and educators to develop metacognitive strategies and efficient academic activities to gain and promote diversity awareness. This practice can make it easier for all to understand that their cultural perspective or perceptions are not universal (Barnhardt, 2014; Guerra & Nelson, 2007).

When educators assertively understand their students' challenges, behaviors, and learning patterns, they help them meet their expectations (Burdett & Crossman, 2012). For instance, the inquirer in the current study, who grew up in Haiti, was taught in grade school that school leaders and professors were his extended parents and his classmates were his best friends for life. He was constantly reminded not to ever criticize his educators, whether they were right or wrong. It was considered disrespectful to make eye contact with or stare at educators. Such behaviors were punishable at home and at school. Physical punishment and other disciplinary actions by both parents and educators were allowed.

Two decades ago, the researcher immigrated to the United States and began interacting with people from different nationalities and cultural background at school, church, work, and other common areas. School became the means for his multicultural education and integration; however, coming from a culture where educators always have the final answers, where educators have complete control of the learning environment and situations, and where students are not encouraged to work in groups and are not supposed to initiate any communication while educators are teaching, to find himself in a school environment that encourage students' active participation, interdependence, and the quality of exchanges between educators, students, and parents, the researcher was quick to assume that the American education was poor and did not meet his expectations. The researcher could not understand that different cultures have different views on learning environments, learning styles, norms, and expectations. It was not enough to quickly learn the language, the customs, and the norms to facilitate his integration. The researcher needed the tools to understand, accept, adapt, and identify himself with the cultural values of his new country, and the educators had to be able to mediate and motivate (Barnhardt, 2014; Ladson-Billings, 2002).

In grade school, the inquirer had to remain silent during lecture unless he was called upon to answer questions or share his ideas. As a student, the inquirer, who grew up in a highly individualist education environment, was to respectfully sit, actively listen, and memorize information. Furthermore, some basic instructional practices like team activities or group activities were not encouraged. Students had to focus on themselves. As the popular saying goes in all classrooms: "Every man for himself and God for all." Students had to abide by it or risk severe punishment. Individualism, personal initiative, competitiveness, and self-assertiveness were the norms.

Understanding of complex cultural issues and appropriate management of differences ensures a foundation for personal, academic, and professional development. Schools are preparing students to live and work in a global environment. These future employees and employers will not have to travel abroad to be in a multicultural environment. It is present within their schools, neighborhoods, and, in some cases, their homes. Diversity is here to stay and grow with society. For the benefit of their students, educators have to lead the way (Kouzes & Posner, 2008; Ladson-Billings, 2002).

Educators need to know their students, their cultural differences, and any challenges they may be encountering, which may include living in a new environment and cultural class, learning a new language, being involved in a new educational environment with different rules, expectations, and teaching systems while they are striving to meet family, community, government expectations, and so forth (Ladson-Billings, 2002). Educators must be able to evaluate their classrooms to discover cultural diversity, develop multicultural programs, and show respect and appreciation of differences while discouraging false assumptions, stereotyping, and ethnocentrism. Multicultural education is a long-term asset to schools, students and their future opportunities, and the global environment. It all begins in the classrooms with the educators (Ladson-Billings, 2009).

Educators can develop a set of preliminary assumptions to help students establish productive intercultural exchanges with teachers and peers. Students need to be encouraged to develop a good understanding of their own cultures and accept themselves as a basic value of their culture (Guerra & Nelson, 2007; Ladson-Billings, 2009). Students need to understand that there is no right or wrong, or better or worse culture while they are being encouraged to value and maintain their sense of authenticity and understand that their cultures are changing just as they grow (Ladson-Billings, 2009). Those concepts enable students to feel acknowledged, appreciated, respected, included, and comfortable with their differences (Guerra & Nelson, 2007). Educators need to infuse multiculturalism into the curriculum to add to their students' comfort in a diverse learning environment. Infusing multicultural interactions in the curriculum can foster students' comfort, skill, and "discourse on difficult topics helping them in developing positive, meaningful, and sustained cross-group relationships" (Lee & Janda, 2006, p. 29; Guerra & Nelson, 2007; Hansuvadha & Slater, 2012; Liua et al., 2008).

"If school administrators do not monitor and model attitudes and practices that promote cultural diversity, then the likelihood of addressing student needs is slim" (Hansuvadha & Slater, 2012, p. 175), which may affect the efficacy of students' learning experiences, the quality of their interactions with others, and the mission of the institution. Cultural awareness does not necessarily rule out any individual beliefs, values, guiding principles, or other cultural components; it only inclines school leaders and educators to teach students to be culturally sensitive, less judgmental, and to value and embrace differences. School leaders need to empower their educators to lead their classrooms (Liua et al., 2008).

Empowering Educators to Lead Their Classrooms

Studies have revealed some significant racial and cultural conflicts between students and minority educators in multicultural institutions. Foreign and other minority educators are considered less competent than white American educators because of their race, their nationalities and linguistic background, and their teaching concepts (Lee & Janda, 2005). Students tend to form biased opinions and negative feelings even before interacting with these educators (Jacobs & Friedman, 1988). In many cases, unfounded stereotypes, preconceived opinions, and negative feelings toward these educators remain the same or become worse throughout the semester, which may affect students' evaluations of the educators and courses (Branch, 2001).

For instance, the inquirer, a foreign-born educator, has been teaching in multicultural environments for over a decade. Over the years, he has experienced multiple students' biased misconceptions at the beginning of most of his classes and in some course evaluation reports. These preconceived negative feelings usually relate to the fact that he is Black, not a native English speaker, and has a foreign linguistic background, with a complete disregard for his experiences, skills, and educational background.

The experiences of the inquirer working in cross-cultural environments have been very enriching. The inquirer has learned many interesting facts about other people and other cultures. These multicultural experiences helped him understand that his cultural views and norms are not universal. Throughout his career he has encountered students from all walks of life. Most of them are immigrants who came to the United States seeking to improve their quality of life through education. Reflecting on his past experiences as a student, the inquirer understands the need to help these students integrate into the American culture without inducing resistance, prejudice, and disrespect toward others.

Sometimes, the inquirer wished other team members and students knew about his cultural differences because, just like others, he believes his cultural background is as important as theirs. Unfortunately, at times, the inquirer had to compromise his cultural values for the greater good of a student, a co-worker, or the institution. The inquirer understood the need to go beyond himself and focus on what everyone has in common. On a few occasions, some students went all the way to administrators and requested a replacement because they felt that the accent of the inquirer hindered their learning. This phenomenon could have fostered some lower evaluation ratings of the educator despite his competence and the richness of the diverse perspectives that he brought to his classrooms, and those students failed to appreciate that unique learning opportunity (Barnhardt, 2014; Branch, 2001).

Schools are the leading force with the power and resources to advocate and implement multiculturalism. It is ideal for respect, freedom, social justice, equity, human dignity, and other social and democratic ideals in their classrooms as well as society (Branch, 2001). Orwin (1996), referring to the value of multiculturalism, opined: "Those who do not love it bear it, and those who accuse it are few. It defines the core of the moral mission of the contemporary" (p. 1). To successfully implement those ideals, leaders of multicultural institutions should seek to recruit and retain educators and scholars with diverse cultural background and develop policies and strategies to help them overcome all biased perceptions and unfair treatment and judgments of their qualifications from their students (Achinstein & Athanases, 2005).

Leaders are expected to have the ability to set the course for sustainable personal and professional growth and development of their environment. That is their highest calling (Maxwell, 1995). Employee empowerment is a necessary and effective management tool for both professional and individual growth (Daft, 2008; Maxwell, 1995). Leaders must provide their subordinates with both tangible and intangible resources not to only perform their assigned duties but also the support and freedom to take initiative, give feedback, and discretion to ensure a leadership role (Maxwell, 1995; Schaubroeck, Lam, & Cha, 2007). An empowered team member may develop a strong sense of commitment, respect, and responsibility toward the success of his or her organization (Gill, Fitzgerald, Bhutani, Mand, & Sharma, 2010).

Professors, as leaders in their classrooms, need to feel empowered to influence and effectively control their environment. It is a valuable motivational management tool. Empowerment encourages professors to strive for even greater self-determination. Transformational leaders acknowledge, inspire, develop, and challenge their followers to become committed leaders as they expand their capabilities and grow (Gill et al., 2010). Razak, Darmawan, and Keeves (2010) suggested the following main reasons why the commitment of a teacher or a professor matters:

> First, commitment was an internal force coming from within teachers themselves who had needs for greater responsibility, variety, and challenge in their work as their level of initial education had grown. Second, there were external forces coming from the educational reform movements seeking higher standards and greater accountability that required teachers' sustained efforts and their commitment to their students, their schools and their work as teachers. (Razak et al., 2010, p. 187)

Empowering subordinates does not necessarily mean that leaders have to shirk their leadership responsibilities; however, delegating responsibilities is a leadership quality and a significant business opportunity they have to value (Gill et al., 2010). Of course, mistakes will be made from time to time, though as Bennis (1994) stated, "as weather shapes mountains, so problems make leaders" (p. 146). In empowering subordinates, leaders encourage their employees to transcend differences, become committed team players, and "use their intelligence to overcome obstacles" (Gill et al., 2010, p. 270).

While empowering followers, leaders must remain in control because it takes leaders and their followers to meet all personal and organizational goals. Klein (1989) suggested leaders can use "control theory" as their integrating framework. Control theory incorporates multiple motivational approaches, which include cognitive process, feedback, goal-setting, and expectancy and attribution theories (Daft, 2008; Klein, 1989). Control theory can enable leaders to encourage their followers to show their skills and their hearts, as leaders, on the other hand, continue to lead and energize followers through a shared vision and purpose. Multiculturalism requires leaders to identify personal and organizational values, value personal talents, develop cultural richness, and empower their followers (Klein, 1989).

Furthermore, while empowering their followers, effective leadership practices involve cognitive approaches. "Cognitive approaches are preferences that are not necessarily rigid, but most people tend to have only a few preferred habits. One of the most widely recognized cognitive differences is between what we call left-brained versus right-brained thinking patterns" (Daft, 2008, p. 114). The cognitive approach emphasizes feedback, which both leaders and their followers need (Daft, 2008, p. 114). As Maxwell (1995) contended, "people need feedback, especially early in their development" (p. 81). "An honest mentor will be objective. If necessary, he or she will encourage the person to stay on course, to seek another direction or even to enter into a relationship with another mentor" (Maxwell, 1995, p. 81).

CHAPTER THREE

METHODOLOGY

Researchers conduct studies to collect information regarding a claim or hypothesis and find answers to their questions (Creswell, 2009; Kumar, 2011; Merriam, 2009). The philosophical orientation of the researcher "may stem from one of the several paradigms and approaches in research – positivist, interpretive, phenomenology, action or participatory, feminist, qualitative, quantitative – and the academic discipline in which you have been trained" (Kumar, 2011, p. 5). Each methodology (i.e., qualitative, quantitative, and mixed) has its purpose, strengths, and weaknesses. They involve both significant differences and similarities (Creswell, 2009; Kumar, 2011; Moustakas, 1994).

Research Design

The qualitative phenomenological approach was best suited for this study because the researcher focused on using an ongoing process to discover, explore, and understand the daily experiences, behaviors, perceptions, and feelings of the participants (Kumar, 2011; Merriam, 2009; Moustakas, 1994). The study was flexible. It continued to develop throughout the procedure (Creswell, 2009; Merriam, 2009; Moustakas, 1994).

Research Question

What are the lived experiences of a diverse group of educators in their multicultural classrooms and the leadership practices developed within their institution?

Research Participants

The researcher individually approached 15 professors from the research site and openly discussed the research topic and the plan of the study with them. After those individual meetings, 10 participants (seven women and three men) were selected based on their differences in terms of personal and cultural background and nationalities, their experiences, and their knowledge in their field and on the subject matter. Participants had worked in the same institution for a minimum of at least 1 year. Participants had previous experience working in multicultural environments before joining their current institution. More than three of the participants held a leadership position. Table 4 provides a demographic representation of the participants by number of years with their current institution, gender, and type of cultural status of their origin countries (monocultural and polycultural environments).

Table 1

Participant Demographics

Participant	Gender	Average Years with Institution	Cultural Status of Original Country
1	M	8	Monoculture
2	M	7	Polyculture
3	F	8	Monoculture
4	F	7	Polyculture
5	F	5	Monoculture
6	F	8	Polyculture
7	F	1	Polyculture
8	M	5	Monoculture
9	F	6	Polyculture
10	F	10	Polyculture

All 10 participants participated in the individual interviews; however, only six participated in the focus group interview. Three participants voluntarily withdrew due to their job status and because they did not want to discuss some of the questions in a group setting. The inquirer purposefully did not invite one participant to participate for fear that her job status could influence other participants' contributions and answers to the study. The inquirer purposefully decided not to document the country of origin of the participants in order to protect their confidentiality as discussed with the participants.

Research Instrumentation

Upon the approval of the institutions and the participants, the researcher began the data collection process using the following instrumentation: (a) one unstructured individual interview; (b) one unstructured focus group session with six of the participants; and (c) a reflective research journal to help the researcher come to terms with his bias and to document spoken words, nonverbal gestures, and other forms of information from the participants throughout the study (Merriam, 2009). Data collection took place within the participants' working environment. The site was selected because it was the natural setting of the participants, which enabled the researcher to collect the most amount of data in the least amount of time.

The researcher sought to immerse himself in the world of the participants to objectively take in what they offered in the interviews, which primarily focused on the research question (DeMarrais, 2004; Denzin & Lincoln, 2011; Merriam, 2009; Patton, 2002). The researcher needed to hear the voices of the participants because he did not know and could not assume how participants organized their environment and personal experiences and the meanings that they attached to them (Denzin & Lincoln, 2011; Merriam, 2009; Patton, 2002).

During the individual interviews, the researcher encouraged flexibility, spontaneity, and freedom in content and structure to enable open exchanges between the participants and the researcher and the participants and other participants (Kumar, 2011; Watt, 2007). The researcher avoided debating and arguing participants' answers regardless of how antithetical the information was with regard to the researcher's personal knowledge, experiences, feelings, and beliefs (Locke, Silverman, & Spriduso, 2010). The researcher maintained neutrality (Merriam, 2009; Watt, 2007). The researcher asked probing questions whenever there was a need to ask for more details, more clarity, or some significant examples. That approach resulted in more effective data collection and data analysis (Grambrill, 2006; Locke et al., 2010; Merriam, 2009).

After the individual interviews that lasted about 60 minutes each, the researcher conducted a 90-minute focus group with six of the participants to collect more data related to the research question and the preliminary emerging themes from the literature review and individual interviews. The inquirer intended to have all 10 participants involved in the focus group interview; however, three participants decided not to participate because they had concerns about discussing some of the research questions in the focus group. They did not feel comfortable revealing themselves to the other participants. Furthermore, the researcher decided not to have one of the participants involved in the focus group because of the leadership role of that participant at the research site.

Participants were unaware of the other participants in the study until they met in the focus group. Participants met in a secured and friendly environment. Before the meeting, participants spoke about different daily personal and professional issues. The inquirer, once again, discussed with participants the objectives of the study, participants' rights and expectations, and their roles and the need for that form of data collection. The inquirer promised the utmost protection of confidentiality.

To begin the focus group, the inquirer shared with participants the preliminary analysis and findings from the literature review and from the individual interviews and invited participants to discuss and make sure that they reflected their responses. Contrary to the in-depth interviews, in the focus group participants were able to interact with the researcher and co-participants. By listening to others, participants became more informed, which encouraged some of them to provide more information while others spoke less than they did in the individual interviews. The focus group was also used as a way to verify responses from the individual interviews (Merriam, 2009; Patton, 2002).

All six participants showed considerable interest in the focus group. They were engaged and expressive throughout the focus group. They expressed themselves both verbally and nonverbally to show interest, disagreement, and agreement with mutual respect. Although participants expressed the same sense of understanding of the research question and topic, there were some similarities and differences in terms of their behaviors and their answers during the focus group, as highlighted in the findings summary. Interviews were recorded on an audio-video device.

The researcher documented his observations throughout the interviews as a third form of data collection in his reflective journal (Creswell, 2009). The researcher also documented participants' actions and gestures and his personal bias, which enabled reflexivity and data reliability; it conveyed the subjectivity of the researcher and trustworthiness and credibility of the study (Creswell, 2009; Locke et al., 2010). Reflexivity, which is "the process of reflecting critically on self as researcher" (Lincoln & Guba, 2000, p. 183), was not an alternative to the researcher's voice in this study. The researcher acknowledged the limits of his reflexivity and was accountable for these limits (Creswell, 2009; Gilgun, 2010; Smith, 2006).

The inquirer developed a set of open-ended questions to let the study emerge (Denzin & Lincoln, 2011; Merriam, 2009). The following questions formed the framework of the individual interviews and the focus group:

- Considering your experiences, what are some advantages and disadvantages in working in a cross-cultural environment?
- What do you wish your co-workers knew about your cultural background, personal and professional experiences which could benefit you and others?
- Tell me about a situation where you had to compromise your cultural values or beliefs in order to avoid or manage any conflict in your workplace.
- How does your cultural background affect your behavior?
- Have your experiences changed your attitude and increased your awareness of diversity? If yes, how? If no, why not?
- How easy or difficult has it been for you to accept differences from others?
- How would a multicultural education development program affect your professional experiences?
- As leader of your classroom (s), what have you done to develop diversity awareness and tolerance in your classrooms?

- How does your relationship with your leader (s) affect your contribution and commitment to your workplace?

The researcher asked more questions as the interviews evolved. Merriam (2009) suggested that "neither the exact wording nor the order of the questions is determined ahead of time" (p. 90). The interview process was tacitly flexible (Kumar, 2011). To facilitate the interviews, the researcher used common or everyday language and avoided asking ambiguous questions, leading questions, or questions based on presumptions; instead, the researcher made every effort to help participants clearly understand the questions, so they could provide relevant information (Kumar, 2011).

Rigor and Validity

The researcher considered rigor and validity to be critical for the authenticity of the study. The value and authenticity of a study are ensured by establishing the following four research components:
- *Credibility.* The integrity of the study is established and shown.
- *Transferability.* The findings of the study can be applied to other contexts.
- *Dependability.* All the procedures of the study are transparent.
- *Confirmability.* The researcher must be able to produce evidence that all procedures took place as described (Creswell, 2009; Kumar, 2011; Merriam, 2009).

The researcher developed a well-structured and rigorous process to establish the authenticity and ethical credibility of the study (Creswell, 2009). The researcher strictly followed the guiding principles established by the Institutional Review Board (IRB) of Argosy University and the research committee of the of the research site. Upon the approval of both institutions, the researcher addressed an informed consent form to all participants, which they were asked to voluntarily sign and return upon their agreement.

The consent form informed participants of their contribution to the study. The consent letter provided detailed information about the relevance of the study and its nature to help participants understand what was expected of them and the responsibility of the researcher (Creswell, 2009). The consent form also explained, in simple terms, the data collection instrumentation and data analysis procedures. It included a concrete description of potential risks, implementation of ethical standards to ensure participants' right to privacy, and the dissemination of the findings (Creswell, 2009; Kumar, 2011).

Furthermore, participants were instructed of their rights to review any data collected throughout the study and after the findings. All participants remained anonymous until they met at the focus group session. To ensure effective data protection and privacy ethical guidelines, all consent forms and data collected were kept confidential, stored in a locked file cabinet and a password protected computer as they came in, and were processed as soon as possible. Only the researcher had access to the filing cabinet (Creswell, 2009; Kumar, 2011; Merriam, 2009).

Methodological Assumptions

This study was based on several assumptions. The qualitative phenomenological method was used because the researcher sought to study the perceptions of the participants of their lived experiences in their natural setting (Creswell, 2009). The data collection and data analysis instruments selected to more effectively enable the researcher to acquire invaluable insight and more in-depth understanding of the phenomenon. The literature review played a large role in the study. The researcher used credible sources; however, there was no way for the researcher to be certain of the credibility of all resources. There could be gaps in the existing literature, and data were self-collected, self-reported, and not independently verified (Creswell, 2009).

Methodological Limitations

The researcher anticipated some limitations to the study. The researcher used a convenient sample that was relatively small (i.e., 10 participants). All participants and the researcher were affiliated with the institution (i.e., research site) during the study. There were possibilities for conflict of interest (Creswell, 2009; Merriam, 1998). The study was conducted in a natural setting, which can be difficult to replicate. The findings cannot be generalized to institutions, similar situations, or other people (Wiersma, 2000). These limitations were inherent in this phenomenological study; however, the researcher managed to minimize the limitations by not letting his frame of reference and his worldview influence the study and its findings (Merriam, 1998; Pedersen, Draguns, Lonner, & Trimble, 2008).

Data Analysis

Data analysis is the process qualitative researchers use to consolidate, reduce, and interpret the data to make sense of them in relation to the research question (Merriam, 2009). After collecting the data, the researcher developed a coding format to prepare and organize the data collected to reduce them to different themes or categories (Creswell, 2009). This process helped the researcher better understand the data and develop research procedures that were compatible with the respondents' information and worldviews and the research topic (Bernard & Ryan, 2010; Kumar, 2011).

Over the years, different coding methods have been developed to help qualitative researchers methodically organize and analyze the overwhelming amount of data collected during research. There is no best specific way to organize data (Bernard & Ryan, 2010; Kumar, 2011). Thus, the researcher had the freedom to creatively use the coding approaches that best fit the needs of this particular study. Qualitative researchers can simply mark segments of data using any type of symbol, category name, descriptive word, or color to organize and divide their data into meaningful analytical units to help them systematically analyze their raw data during or after the data collection phase (Bernard & Ryan, 2010; Creswell, 2009; Kumar, 2011).

As the researcher was going through the interview transcripts, he assigned a unique coding symbol to signify any particular segment as he saw fit to the research question, the literature review, and the interviews. The researcher continued the process until he segmented all data. The quality of the coding format impacted both the efficiency of the analysis of the data and the accuracy of the findings. As Strauss (1987) and Merriam (2009) suggested, the researcher developed research questions to define a human phenomenon and collect a purposeful sample to study the phenomenon, but the research findings were shaped by the data collected and analysis that went with the process.

The researcher generated a preliminary codebook to code the data (Creswell, 2009; Merriam, 2009). As the coding and analysis phases progressed, both manually and electronically, if any error or misunderstanding was suspected the researcher went back to his transcripts, his reflective journal, his marginal notes, or to the respondents for confirmation and approval instead of editing the data (Kumar, 2011; Moustakas, 1994). Data analysis is an ongoing process; during the analysis process, the researcher was involved in a constant discovery process and deeper immersion into the data (Hennink, Hutter, & Bailey, 2011; Moustakas, 1994).

CHAPTER FOUR

RESULTS

This chapter contains a summary of the findings from both the individual and focus group interviews. The researcher used a qualitative method to study the overreaching research question: What are the lived experiences of a diverse group of educators in their multicultural classrooms and the leadership practices developed within their institution?

Interview questions were developed based on the research question and previous literature pertaining to the openness of leaders of multicultural schools to cultural diversity, organizational conflicts, multicultural leadership, multicultural education and development, affirming diversity, leader-member exchange, transformational leadership, and team empowerment.

Individual and Focus Group Responses

The researcher developed a set of nine open-ended questions pertaining to the overreaching research question and the literature review. Other questions were addressed to establish clarity or for further details. After the data collection process, the researcher transcribed all data from the audio-video device and analyzed his reflective journal to facilitate the interpretation and data analysis steps. The researcher rigorously analyzed and interpreted all the positive and negative aspects of the responses from both the individual and focus group interviews and the reflective journal, which was used to establish triangulation of sources. Such practices enabled the discovery of the significant themes of the study, which are relevant to the literature review (Merriam, 2009).

Question 1

Considering your experiences, what are some advantages and disadvantages in working in your cross-cultural institution?

Participant 1 have been with the institution for more than 5 years and had taught for more 10 years in two different countries. He suggested he would always choose to work in a multicultural environment because such an environment offers more personal and professional advantages to succeed in the multicultural American society. He stated:

> I don't really see anything that I could consider as disadvantage. There is so much one can do as an educator when working in a multicultural educational institution. When you are in multicultural learning environment, it is all about a learning process for both educators and students. Teachers and students are learning from each other.

Participant 2 grew up in a multicultural environment and had years of experiences working in a multicultural environment. He had worked with the institution for more than 5 years. He acknowledged that multiculturalism has some advantages, such as the opportunity to increase multicultural competency, higher levels of teamwork, and cooperation in working with individuals from different cultural background who have different personal and professional experiences, perspectives, and approaches. On the other hand, he also acknowledged some disadvantages of multicultural diversity. He shared that "one of the biggest disadvantages of cross-cultural workforces is cross cultural barriers; individuals' perceptions, stereotypes, and misconceptions about other cultural groups can lead to frustration and misunderstanding if communication is not maintained."

Participant 3 agreed that working in a multicultural environment can be both advantageous and disadvantageous depending on the meaning that leaders and employees of the institution add to multicultural diversity. She said advantages include the cross-cultural sharing and idea generation and ultimate growth that come with working with individuals from different cultures. She said: "In a multicultural environment, one gets to learn something new every day. However, how that knowledge or experience is perceived by individuals is significant." She admitted that some disadvantages include, first and foremost, ignorance and prejudicial misconceptions of other cultures and individuals, which can lead to critical tasks and individual conflicts.

Participant 4 said that she grew up in a mono-cultural society. She believed that teaching in a multicultural environment is challenging. She claimed her experience taught her to be open while learning about other cultures, ways of life, languages, and people. Such a conception made it easier for her to expand her horizons with more opportunities. Her success in a multicultural environment was related to her level of sensitivity to, acknowledgment of, and tolerance for cultural diversity.

Participant 5 acknowledged the need to value cultural differences and advocate for multiculturalism for the greater good of educators and their students. She said:

> I have the opportunity to learn a lot about people, their cultural background, their lived experiences, and many more. The way they behave, interact with others, and respond to certain situations in my classrooms, is an amazing life-learning process of people. Working in this multicultural environment has helped me a lot in developing my multicultural competency. I have not realized any disadvantages whatsoever. I understand that multiculturalism has some considerable trends; however, those changes are more like lessons to learn and understand that I transform into social, professional, and personal opportunities. I have learned to remain open-minded, supportive, and culturally sensitive to acknowledge, respect, tolerate, and live with differences.

Participant 6 grew up in a multicultural society. She had worked with the institution for over five years. She witnessed how the department grew to become very diverse. She suggested she had the opportunity to meet colleagues and students from different parts of the world, which made her work environment very interesting. She shared she had become more culturally competent. She learned something new every day. She added:

> The excitement that I have gotten from working in this environment has encouraged me to travel abroad, which has been very helpful for my

personal and professional lives. Working in this multicultural environment has not shown any disadvantages about multiculturalism. I am working with other professors from Europe and other American countries. I have been exposed to major differences and some difficulties to accept them; however, I accept them and use them as advantages to be a better professor. I see those professors have different ways of teaching English, and I am learning a lot from them.

Participant 7 worked for more than 10 years in different multicultural education institutions. She acknowledged that from her extended experience, there was a constant need to affirm diversity in a diverse school environment. She said that if well-managed, multiculturalism can be all about advantages. She added: "It is significant to be able to expand one's professional environment with a global mindset because globalization is no longer a distant affair. It is right in the classrooms, on the campuses, and in the neighborhood."

Participant 8 worked in many multicultural education institutions. In defining the advantages and disadvantages of working in multicultural institutions, he said:

My experience has taught me that working in a multicultural environment offers all advantages for one to learn to acknowledge, accept, and appreciate others even more. Multiculturalism may start with differences but lead to meaningful inclusion. Our cultural differences may be counted as disadvantages, but I know that everyone matters and has something to offer to create the best working and learning environment for professors and our students. Overall, multiculturalism transforms differences into advantages.

Participant 9 lived in different countries. She said that growing up in a multicultural household has a major impact on how she perceived multiculturalism and its advantages. She made the case that there was no need for her to focus on disadvantages when it came to working in a multicultural institution. She said:

> A major advantage of multiculturalism is you get the best results. For example, when one looks at anything from all 360 degrees of a circle and consider all prospective, you have all possibility to get the best result. Many times if you do not have different ways to look at the same thing, you do not have the advantage of having so many different ideas to consider, and you may miss the best. Diversity offers the opportunity to have the best. Multiculturalism also has some trends. It takes time, patience, sacrifice, and education to make it work.

Participant 10 is from a multicultural urban population. She has lived and worked in different countries and educational institutions for over 10 years. She suggested that there are keen advantages and disadvantages to working in multicultural environments. She said she found it interesting to work with people with varied cultural background. She learned and interacted with others in unique ways because many of her colleagues and students were culturally and linguistically diverse. She also claimed that she was constantly challenged in interesting ways to be understood and understand. She also highlighted some disadvantages. She opined:

> There can be more misunderstandings and misinterpretations, usually of the kind where someone feels as if they've been disrespected or put down. I think that the students feel very different because they are not speaking their first language, and they can be hypersensitive when interacting with people speaking English. Also, there is a lot of stereotyping going on. I understand that this is how both students and faculty manage diverse environments, but I really feel uncomfortable with sweeping generalizations about others.

Question 1 investigated the advantages and disadvantages in working in a multicultural setting. Given their responses pertaining to their experiences, all participants highlighted the many advantages they came upon. Some of those advantages included the numerous learning opportunities to increase their diversity competency, become more academically creative for better productivity, develop new attitudes while developing a global mindset, and eliminating their prejudices. On the other hand, some participants highlighted some disadvantages of multiculturalism. They mentioned issues involving communication barriers, cultural resistance, discrimination, increased cost, conflicts, and unproductivity. Table 2 highlights the fundamental themes that emerged from the responses of the participants.

Table 2

Question 1 Emergent Themes

Theme	Responses from Participants
Advantages of Multiculturalism	Multicultural environment . . . offers more personal and professional advantages to succeed.

It is all about a learning process for both educators and students.

The opportunity to increase multicultural competency, higher levels of teamwork and cooperation.

One gets to learn something new every day.

Working in . . . multicultural environment has helped . . . in developing my multicultural competency.

The opportunity of meeting colleagues and students from different parts of the world.

Multiculturalism is all about advantages.

Multiculturalism may start with differences but lead to meaningful inclusion. |

Theme	Responses from Participants
	You get the best result. Interesting to work with people with varied cultural background.
Disadvantages of Multiculturalism	One of the biggest disadvantages of cross cultural workforces is cross cultural barriers; individuals' perceptions, stereotypes, and misconceptions about other cultural groups can lead to frustration and misunderstanding if communication is not maintained. First and foremost, ignorance and prejudicial misconceptions of other cultural and individuals, which can lead to critical tasks and individual conflicts. Teaching in a multicultural environment is challenging. Multiculturalism has some considerable trends. Our cultural differences may be counted as disadvantages. It takes time, patience, sacrifice, and education to make it work. There can be more misunderstandings and misinterpretations.

Table 2 continued

Question 2

What do you wish your co-workers knew about your cultural background, personal and professional experiences which could benefit you and others?

Participant 1 took a deep breath before answering the question. He said he found it hard to talk about himself but acknowledged the need to do so. He said one way to help limit misjudgment, stereotyping, and false cultural assumptions was to openly let others know who he was. Then he added:

> I wish my colleagues knew that I am not a judge. I embrace diversity with open arms. I reject cultural stereotyping, cultural labeling. I would like for my colleagues not to see me or interact with me because of any sort of cultural conceptions. I would like for them to know me. They should value everything I can contribute for the greater good of the team which may have nothing to do with my cultural background. I understand that I joined the institution with my background; however, I have managed not to let my cultural background to influence my position and my roles in my working environment.

Participant 2 was quick to say that people work better and interact better with others because they know each other. However, he suggested the following:

> I believe a certain amount of humility and privacy should exist in relationships with others. I don't want to reveal my own or know the innermost personal experiences of everyone with whom I interact. Trust and respect are built over time and

through an individual's actions, and when the time is right personal and professional experiences can be revealed to enhance a relationship or explain a particular attitude. Participant 2 said: "I want my colleagues and my students to know that I have strong work ethic." He tended to stay at work until the job was done. He focused on the job but not on the work hours. He liked to spend long hours trying to improve his knowledge, plan his classes, and grade papers. He added that he had a "can do and will do" attitude. Within reason, he craved perfection. He also wanted his colleagues to know that he believed the effect of cultural differences could be reduced and a more harmonious workplace could exist by establishing norms of behavior.

Participant 3 found the question interesting and necessary, but she wondered how much was too little or too much when it came to sharing personal and cultural information with colleagues. She said she did not know whether it was possible or important to learn or share personal experiences and cultural differences with others. She said:

I do not think it would make that much of a difference if people knew I was married to a Frenchman my family called the terrorist because he looked Middle Eastern or that my Republican father said he wouldn't be seen in public with my second husband and me because he was from Brazil and darker skinned. They are just stories of reality, stories that each one of us can share. I think that what is more important is that human beings from all cultures look at one another as equals. The cultural filters and prejudices are the problems that create differences versus oneness. Oneness is what we must all come to.

Some participants elaborated on the question, but Participant 4 did not say much. She was simple and direct. She only wanted others to know that she was from a multicultural environment, and she was aware of many multicultural trends that could be either beneficial or detrimental to personal and professional lives.

Participant 5 wanted her colleagues to know that she grew up in a mono-cultural environment. She is very conservative, and she religiously identifies with her cultural background. She added:
> I grew up in an environment that is very socially different from the western countries. Even the clothes that I wear reflect certain social norms of my country. Of course, I have been living in the United States for quite some time; however, I still feel it invaluable to identify myself with my cultural background.

She said she was still making baby steps when it came to being and working in a multicultural environment. She claimed that professors in her country were highly respected and valued, and students and other members of the community had high expectations of them.

Participant 6 decided to only focus on her religious belief to answer the question. She said she found it more valuable than any other cultural dimensions. She said:" I wish my co-workers knew that I am a very religious person, and I would not accept to do anything to compromise my religious belief. I grew up in an environment that unconditionally values religious practices." Furthermore, she added:

> It really hurt when I was asked to work on my religious holidays. I was not given any option. I was basically told that I had to. Well, I was not happy. I felt disrespected; however, I understood that I did not have a choice. I worked on that day. I still do not like the fact that my expectation was not met. Later on, I discussed it with my leader; then I realize it was not personal. Over the years, I have learned to go beyond my personal interests for the greater good of my institution. I was just needed, and I had to be there for the team. After all, I am a team player.

Participant 7 wanted her colleagues to acknowledge and accept her for her commitment and contribution to her department. She argued that "I do not like when others tend to identify me with others from my country or any biased cultural dimension." She wanted others to know that she welcomes diversity, and she was ready to develop her multicultural competency.

Participant 8 would like his colleagues to know that he was from a very mono-cultural environment and he was still learning to develop his multicultural competency. He also mentioned:

> I would like for my co-workers to know that I am from a very goal-oriented culture. Back in my country, we learn that people must have goals. The quality of our goals defines the quality of our

lives. We identify and measure ourselves with our goals.

Participant 9 claimed that others usually tend to mistake her ethnic background assuming she is Hispanic, which is something she does not appreciate. She said:

> I would like for my colleagues to know that I am from Hispanic background that I am so proud of; however, I had the opportunity to grow up in an only English speaking household. I understand that I do not interact too much with my co-workers; however, I would like for them to know that I am not antisocial. I like people.

Question 2 addressed the issue of self-acknowledgment and what participants wished others knew about them. Participants answered by explaining how personally they valued and understood their individuality in terms of cultural background, personality traits, capability, behavior, shortcomings, prejudices, likes and dislikes, and expectations. All participants agreed that they brought their whole selves into their institution. They admitted they had not disclosed themselves enough despite the fact that they knew their self-disclosure would be beneficial to their workplace because it would foster better relationships with others and organizational productivity. Table 3 shows the emergent theme from participants' responses.

Table 3

Question 2 Emergent Theme

Theme	Responses of Participants
Importance of Self-Acknowledgment	I embrace diversity with open arms. I wish my colleagues knew that I am not a judge. I . . . have strong work ethic. I wish my co-workers knew that I am a very religious person, and I would not accept to do anything to compromise my religious belief. I do not like when others tend to identify me with others from my country or any biased cultural dimension. I am far from perfect. I am from a very goal-oriented culture. I would like for my colleagues to know that I am from Hispanic background that I am so proud of. Everything about me is a reflection of my upbringing.

Question 3

Tell me about a situation where you had to compromise your cultural values or beliefs in order to avoid or manage any conflict in your workplace.

Participant 1 suggested conflict is imminent everywhere. He never had to compromise his cultural values or beliefs to avoid or manage any conflict in his work setting. He usually managed to go beyond cultural background and differences. He said:

> I like to meet others halfway without compromising my beliefs and some of my guiding principles. I learn to focus on the greater good of all or the institution because, regardless of the nature of the cultural conflict, our priority is the institution. So, working to find a common ground is the most important.

Participant 2 shared the view of Participant 1. He agreed that conflict is inevitable when individuals work together regardless of their culture and personal and professional background because people have different personal and professional experiences, ideas, and methods of achieving objectives. Furthermore, he explained:

> In principle, I do not compromise my cultural values or beliefs. I do not think I should or have to; however, I am always open to see another individual's point of view, and I am willing to negotiate a resolution which leaves all parties with mutually beneficial results. I prefer to avoid compromising situations by keeping lines of communication open and proactive, dealing with

conflict quickly and openly, and not looking for blame or getting personal about sensitive issues.

Participant 3 decided not to answer the question. She mentioned that she could not think of one specific task or personal conflict in which she was involved at work. She understood that conflict could surface at any time. Regardless of the situation, she managed to avoid or effectively solve it without compromising her values.

Participant 4 found it difficult not to reflect on her cultural background when dealing with some personal or task conflict at work. She tended to follow and reinforce school policy.

Participant 5 also acknowledged that she had not been exposed to any type of conflict at her workplace. She said that she understood that it could come up at any time. Therefore, she was ready to face it with an open mind, no assumption, and no cultural bias. She stated:

> Of course, I know that I am not going to compromise my values or principles. I may choose some non-popular approaches to face that challenge for the greater good those involved; however, I tend to enforce or re-enforce the institution policy if necessary. I live by my principles. I identify myself with my principles. I will not compromise my principles. I would not ask or encourage someone to do that either.

Participant 6 used the following incident to answer the question. She explained:

I remember that I came across a co-worker who was exhibiting some gestures that he claimed was demonstrating his openness to diverse sexual orientation. His behavior offended many of his students who came from cultures that reject homosexuality. I approached the professor who became very defensive during the conversation. I did not think that his behavior was professionally and educationally appropriate. I avoided confrontation. I openly and respectfully express my opinion on his behavior, as I would do in any other cultural conflict.

Then she said she would not compromise her cultural values.

Participant 8 faced some cultural conflicts with some students. He shared the following:

I have faced some culture conflicts with some students. I have managed to solve them without compromising my values. I would not compromise my guiding principles. When problems come, I only have to implement effective problem solving skills and school policies to overcome them. All begins with a good understanding and an effective assessment of the problem. Most of the conflicts that I have been involved in are mostly matters of misunderstanding and misconception, and false cultural assumptions.

Participant 9 claimed she had never been directly involved in any cultural conflict at work. Then she shared the following story:

> I remember when someone made a derogatory comment about someone. It was a backhanded compliment. That person said: "He is so smart, but it's too bad he does not have lighter skin." It was shocking to hear that from my work environment. Unfortunately, I did not address the comment assertively, which I should have. I was just too shocked.

She said that the situation happened a long time ago; however, she still felt bad because she did not do anything.

Participant 10 admitted that as difficult as it was, she always managed not to let her cultural values or her differences affect her decision-making approach. She shared the story of the following incident:

> I had one employee accused another of sexual harassment. The other employee was wrong in that he closed the office door and yelled in her face. She, not a native speaker of English, interpreted his closing the door to "talk" as an overt sexual threat. She took the charge to HR. Both met and she could not see the events as anything but sexual harassment. He was flabbergasted, and both felt victimized. He was made to apologize to her, and what she had done that had caused him to yell at her was never part of the resolution of this conflict. I had to abide by that, and it felt unfair and almost as if she was abusing the phrase to cover up her mistake. On the other hand, I'm not sure if this was a lingual/cultural misunderstanding.

Enacting diversity brings both benefits and challenges, which can increase conflict. Question 3 investigated whether participants had experienced cultural conflict at work and approaches they had developed, in terms of compromising their cultural values, to effectively manage or avoid those conflicts. Some participants admitted they had not experienced any form of cultural conflict at work. Few of the participants had faced some conflicts they believed were culturally related. In all cases, participants acknowledged the correlations between their responsibilities, organizational policies, and their guiding principles. As their responses show in Table 4, all participants agreed they deeply ascribed to their values because they were the essence of their existence. They would not compromise their values.

Table 4

Question 3 Emergent Theme

Theme	Responses of Participants
Cultural Conflict	Individuals' perceptions, stereotypes, and misconceptions about other cultural groups can lead to frustration and misunderstanding. I have faced some culture conflicts with couple students. There is a lot of stereotyping going on. Conflict is pretty much inevitable when individuals work together. Conflict is imminent everywhere. Ignorance and prejudicial misconceptions of other cultural and individuals . . . can lead to critical tasks and individual conflicts. There can be more misunderstandings and misinterpretations. Everyone is different; every situation is different.

Question 4

How does your cultural background affect your behavior?

Participant 1 stated his cultural background did not really prepare him to work in such a culturally diverse environment; however, the good thing for him was he was from a highly collective social environment.

Working with others and valuing differences were some of his strengths. He acknowledged that his cultural background and the experiences he acquired over the years played major roles in his working behavior and interactions with others.

Participant 2 pointed out that as a culturally aware individual he tended to be able to identify cultural characteristics and usually managed to relate to them to meet organizational goals and expectations. Like Participant 1, he claimed that he understood that his cultural background could always come in to play; however, in some situations, one must understand the need to put cultural and personal differences aside temporarily in order to work together.

Participant 3 saw herself as the product of her cultural background. She stated that her spiritual beliefs and other cultural components were a very big part of how she performed tasks and interacted with others. She made the case that "we are all one." She also suggested that it was from the standpoint of ahimsa, non-violence, or love that she developed interactions with everyone. She acknowledged: "I am far from perfect, yet I strive to remember that the person in front of me is as human as I am."

Participant 4 said that her cultural background strongly impacted her working behavior and interactions with others. She admitted that she was still learning, but it had not been easy observing some cultural behaviors being exhibited by some students and educators. Some of those behaviors were very unacceptable in her culture. She stated:

> I am getting used to people who are not as reserved as people in my country. They are louder, and they use gestures frequently. Also, kissing professors on cheeks in the hallways as a part of greeting is different than what I am used to as well as sharing personal or intimate information with class or teachers.

Participant 5 did not talk about herself. She referred to others from her country. She used the personal pronoun "we" instead of I. She said:

> When it comes to interacting with others, people from other countries usually call people from my country sheep. It is only because we do not really like to argue. We normally use a more peace-making approach. We do not simply stay quiet or just compromise; however, we emphasize common interest in solving problems. We can disagree without being disagreeable with others. In interacting with others and performing our tasks, we are respectful, supportive, helpful, and flexible. Whatever we do reflects our cultural background.

After taking a long time to analyze the question, Participant 6 made the case that her cultural background defines both her working behavior and the quality of her relationship with others. She added that she understood how important it was to be loyal to her institution; however, as she mentioned, "everything about me is a reflection of my upbringing."

Participant 7 declared that "I am who I am, and everything about me reflects my cultural background. However, I find it acceptable to go beyond my cultural background to contribute as much as necessary at work and to build sustainable interactions with others." She added: "I am constantly managing my cultural values, others' differences, and my team's expectations."

Participant 8 said that someone's cultural upbringing and life experiences will always affect his or her interactions with others and his or her work ethic. People only have to learn how to effectively manage in order to meet job objectives, acknowledge, value, and tolerate differences. He concluded with:

> I always try to emphasize common interest or the greater good of all. I was raised in a collectivist social environment where I learned that respecting and accepting others with their differences are significant to build a sustainable community.

Participant 9 shared:
> I have learned from my parents that nothing or nobody is perfect. Over all, my cultural background has taught me that everyone matters. Our differences are positive. Those conceptions define my working behavior and my interactions with others.

Question 4 was designed to investigate the impact of culture on the participants' behaviors in their environment. All participants suggested their cultural background played a prominent role in their behavior in terms of interacting with other people, performing tasks, and making decisions. Some participants acknowledged other factors that influenced their behaviors; however, their values and beliefs were relevant to their assumptions of others and their environments. As they were very outspoken surrounding the importance of their cultures, some participants admitted to their prejudices and some limitations of their cultures when it came to acknowledging and accepting others' differences. Table 5 contains the emergent theme and responses of the participants.

Table 5

Question 4 Emergent Theme

Theme	Responses of Participants
Impact of Culture on Personal Behavior	Cultural background has played major roles on . . . behavior.
	Identify cultural characteristics and usually manages to relate to them to meet organizational goals and expectations.
	Cultural background can always come to play.
	Spiritual beliefs and other cultural components are a very big part . . . when performing . . . tasks.
	I am far from perfect, yet I strive to remember that the person in front of me is as human as I am.
	Cultural background has strongly impacted . . . working behavior.
	Whatever we do reflects our cultural background.
	My cultural background defines both my working behavior and the quality of my relationship with others.
	Everything about me is a reflection of my upbringing.

Theme	Responses of Participants
	I am who I am, and everything about me reflects my cultural background.

Table 5 continued

Question 5

Have your experiences changed your attitude and increased your awareness of diversity? If yes, how? If no, why not?

Participant 1 shared that his experience in his work setting greatly improved his knowledge, attitude, and awareness of cultural diversity. Furthermore, he stated: "being able to work, being able to deal with so many differences, and learning from my students and colleagues who are from other background have been excellent."

Participant 2 estimated that his knowledge and perception of racial and cultural stereotypes had absolutely changed. It has become fascinating for him to discuss and learn about different point of views and opinions with individuals from other cultures. He explained the following: "The more time I spend with individuals from other cultures the more I understand them, and the more similar I realize that we are."

Participant 5 suggested that "after five years of working with students and colleagues from other background, I am happy about the person and professor that I have become." She added that what she learned from her students and her colleagues greatly developed her attitude and awareness of multicultural differences. She shared the following observation of herself and the changes she has made over the years:

> I used to see the world and others only based upon my personal background, experiences, and beliefs. Now, I am happy for being able to see beyond my cultural norms, my beliefs, and my experiences. I see and accept that the world is ours. Our similarities and differences will continue to add more meaning to our multicultural institution and the rest of the world. My workplace has been a great learning environment for me, and I am successfully growing up.

Participant 6 explained that "my attitude has changed, and my awareness of diversity has improved. I understand the need to avoid stereotyping and other forms of cultural misconceptions because they can foster serious conflicts."

Participant 7 made the case that her attitude has changed. Her awareness and her tolerance toward diversity were invaluable opportunities she had been exploring for both personal and professional success.

Participant 8 stated that he had become more sensitive, more aware, and more tolerant. He opined: "I see how much diversity from my colleagues has helped me grow personally and professionally. Every day at work is more like a wonderful adventure around the world, which has helped me avoid stereotyping and false cultural assumptions."

Participant 10 answered simply by saying: "very much so." Then she shared the following:

I found people to be very intolerant of Hispanic students and heard people say terrible things about Blacks and Mexicans. I was shocked because I hadn't been exposed to some of the attitudes and expressions I heard. As a result, I became involved in diversity initiatives and increasing my own cultural competence so that I could help students and colleagues overcome stereotyping.

In Question 5, the researcher wanted to understand whether participants' experiences in their diverse workplace changed their attitudes and increased their awareness of diversity. In both interviews, all participants acknowledged positive changes in their attitudes and noted their awareness of diversity increased. Based on their responses, participants developed strong affirming diversity. They defined diversity as a form of social justice. Their experiences helped them undergo a deep shift in their attitudes, values, prejudices, beliefs, and norms in order to affirm the differences of their students and their colleagues, as shown in Table 6.

Table 6

Question 5 Emergent Theme

Theme	Responses of Participants
Developing Affirming Diversity	Advocate multiculturalism in multicultural institutions.

A culturally aware individual, he tends to be able to identify cultural characteristics and usually manages to relate to them to meet organizational goals and expectations for the greater good of educators and theirs students.

I find my strengths in differences. Difference is very significant. Diversity is richness.

Everyone is different; every situation is different; every culture is unique.

Being able to work, being able to deal with so many differences, and learning from my students and colleagues who are from other background has been excellent.

We are all one.

There is constant need for affirming diversity.

The more time I spend with individuals from other cultures the more I understand them, and the more similar I realize that we are.

Our similarities and differences will continue to add more meaning to our |

Theme	Responses of Participants
	multicultural institution and the rest of the world.
	I understand the need to avoid stereotyping and other forms of cultural misconceptions.
	I see how much diversity from my colleagues have helped me grow personally and professionally. Every day at work is more like travelling around the world.
	I became involved in diversity initiatives.

Table 6 continued

Question 6

How easy or difficult has it been for you to accept differences from others?

When it came to accepting differences, Participant 1 admitted that it was not always easy; however, over the years he had developed some specific approaches that made it easier to accept differences. He stated:

> I understand the need to go beyond my self-interests and my cultural differences to embrace others and what they have to say and do to improve themselves and the environment. At times, it may be difficult to listen to differences; however, I value everyone because together we can come up with better outcomes. I always believe that two sets of eyes can see more than

one set of eyes. I never want my followers to simply accept what I say or my ideas as the rules to strictly accept and follow. I need their input. I value their input. I value their differences.

Participant 4 explained that accepting differences was not easy; however, instead of ignoring differences, she learned to develop her knowledge by asking questions and avoiding forming quick opinions or judgments and managed to accept differences with an open mind.

Accepting differences was a big weakness for Participant 5. She shared:

Now, it is so easy for me to accept differences as long as they are not personally hurtful to me or others. If it hurts, I will not tolerate it. As much as I love to learn about others' cultural background, I learn not to discuss or debate them. I learn it, value it, respect it, and tolerate it.

Participant 6 realized that it had not been difficult for her to accept differences. She stated:

Accepting differences is part of my learning process to become more knowledgeable of others. As I am becoming more culturally competent, I become closer to others and more sensitive and more compassionate. Considering my professional field, it is very important that I listen and learn from others. I realize that my colleagues are different in teaching styles and interactions with their students and other colleagues. I value their differences and their similarities.

Participant 8 answered the question in the following terms:
In the past, it was very challenging for me to accept differences. But, now, I find it easy, acceptable, and beneficial to accept differences. I may not necessary agree with them all; however, I acknowledge them and value them. I believe that, if well-managed, positive differences can become opportunity. I objectively listen to others, and we work together as a team.

Participant 9 believed accepting differences was not always an easy thing to do, but she knew not to value things or ideas only from her personal perspective or experiences. She managed to express considerable respect for differences and others as much as she valued similarities.

Participant 10 shared that accepting differences was not a simple issue. It required a lot of training. She offered the following suggestion: "The biggest and most informative part is to learn how to silence your mind and really listen to others while filtering your own biases."

Question 6 addressed the issue of accepting differences to develop affirming diversity. The inquirer wanted to find out how easy or difficult it was for participants to make those changes in their attitudes. All participants acknowledged that it was not easy to accept differences, but it was worth it because they realized that accepting others could be personally and professional beneficial. Most agreed that it was not an easy choice; however, they acknowledged their expectations of being accepted also with their own differences. Some learned to accept differences by visualizing with a positive mindset as an opportunity instead of an encumbrance. Over the years, they patiently learned to cultivate acceptance of others. Table 7 demonstrates the emergent theme and responses of participants to this question.

Table 7

Question 6 Emergent Theme

Theme	Responses of Participants
Accepting Differences	It is not always easy.
	I reflect on myself.
	Two sets of eyes can see more than one set of eyes.
	Accepting differences was one big weakness.
	I learn it, value it, respect it, and tolerate it.
	Accepting differences is part of my learning process to become more knowledgeable of others.
	As I am becoming more culturally competent, I become closer to others and more sensitive and more compassionate.
	Back then, it was very challenging for me to accept differences. But, now, I find easy, acceptable, and beneficial to accept differences.
	Accepting differences is not a simple issue. It requires a lot of training.
	The biggest and most informative part is to learn how to silence your mind and really listen to others while filtering your own biases.

Question 7

How would a multicultural education development program affect your professional experiences?

Participant 1 stated a multicultural education development program could make him a better person, a better colleague, and a better educator in a multicultural education institution. He added that it would be beneficial to the whole institution.

Participant 2 suggested: "A multicultural education development program would benefit everyone: faculty, students, and administrative personnel."

Participant 3 admitted that she wished she had the opportunity to attend a multicultural development program before she began her teaching career. She added such a program would be extraordinary in bringing people together and creating oneness.

Participant 4 said that a multicultural development program would prepare educators for more awareness, tolerance, and sensitivity toward colleagues and students.

Participant 5 answered the question in the following terms:

> A multicultural education development program would be great. I know that I would learn a lot from such a program. I am still in a multiculturalism learning process. I need it. It

would make me a better person and a more successful educator.

Participant 6 claimed that she went to school to become a professor; however, multicultural education was never a part of the school's curricula. She admitted that a multicultural education development program would be necessary. She realized the difference it would make in her teaching career.

Participant 7 suggested that such a program would benefit everyone, including students, educators, and school leaders.

Participant 8 made the following statement:
A multicultural education program would benefit me a lot. I would enjoy being involved in it. It would help the whole environment. I would become more culturally competent facing cultural challenges. It would make a major difference in my professional and personal lives. Our institution is becoming more diverse every day. We must be ready for the changes and the challenges.

Participant 9 opined that a multicultural education development program would be great. She said that such a program would add to the value of the institution. And participant 10 stated: "It would make this place a better place."

In Question 7, the researcher questioned the importance and need for a multicultural education development for participants in their institution. The question was openly welcomed by all participants. They all needed it and wished it could be offered in their institution. They agreed on its necessity, its importance, and how much they would be willing to participate in such program. Participants discussed the growing need for educators to be culturally educated in order to be effective in a diverse environment. They need to be constantly learning, developing, and demonstrating cultural characteristics to keep in tune with others while reaching across cultures because, as some participants mentioned, it is all about effective human resource development, which their institution could capitalize on (See Table 8).

Table 8

Question 7 Emergent Theme

Theme	Responses of Participants
Need for Professional Multicultural Education Development	That would make it easier . . . to build a much better learning environment for her students with more reasonable expectations.
	Someone is never too prepared for multicultural trends because everyone is different; every situation is different; every culture is unique.
	Multicultural education . . . can only make him a better person, a better colleague, and a better educator in a multicultural education institution.
	A multicultural education development program would benefit everyone: faculty, students, and administrative personnel.
	Multicultural development program would definitely prepare educators for more awareness, tolerance, and sensitivity towards colleagues and students.
	I know that I would learn a lot from such program.
	Multicultural education would be necessary.

Question 8

As leader of your classroom (s), what have you done to develop diversity awareness and tolerance in your classrooms?

Participant 1 acknowledged his role as a leader in developing awareness and tolerance of diversity in his classroom. He shared his approach in the following terms:

> Encouraging, inspiring, and developing tolerance for diversity in my classroom is a daily priority for me. I value my students, and I show respect for my students in order to develop mutual respect. I work with my students to help them develop the environment's value, embrace, and tolerate differences. I lead the way because I know my students are looking up to me. My students come from different parts of the world. I know that they expect to be accepted, valued, and loved regardless of their differences. That approach can definitely make it easier for them to be more involved. That approach makes their learning process very much easier because it empowers them and strengthens their confidence.

Participant 2 explained that professors play a dominant role in helping their students: value, accept, and tolerate differences. He explained:

> I make a point of introducing myself and explaining my background as a method to prime students to do the same. I make sure I know where all my students are from, the languages they speak, and cultural specifics they possess. Additionally, I promote cultural harmony and acceptance by ensuring students are aware of stereotypes, generalizations, and culturally insensitivity when and if they ever use any in my presence. I explain what they have said or done,

how it might be perceived, why it is insensitive, and how to avoid it in the future. I am their bridge builder.

Participant 3 used multiple approaches to develop multicultural diversity awareness in her classrooms. She gave the following account of some practices:

At the beginning of each semester, I always spend time creating an atmosphere where each student feels part of a friendly and safe learning environment. I consistently try to minimize the potential infiltration of any prejudices I might harbor during class activities. I develop activities that emphasize teamwork, which usually make it easier for students to meet, to know, and to learn from each other. Those activities are to help students to learn that they are not so different, but may just be alike in many ways. As their leader, I try to model behavior that begets similar behavior. My one class rule is respect. I am very forthright and will stop class to have a discussion if something harmful/disrespectful has been done. As a class, we will decide what action needs to be taken before the issue gets blown out of proportion. Often a simple discussion/clarification of feelings and filters is enough for everyone to understand why someone behaved the way they did.

Participant 4 established some basic rules to help her students transform the challenges of multicultural diversity into a lifelong education opportunity. She encouraged and inspired her students to openly and respectfully express themselves. She said that she showed no tolerance for discrimination based on race, origin, nationality, gender, age, and other forms of diversity dimensions. She encouraged her students to conduct research and educate themselves about cultural background.

Participant 5 explained that encouraging and developing awareness and tolerance for diversity in her classroom was a priority. She shared the following:

I have integrated diversity in my curricula. I usually start doing it on the first day of class. During my introduction, I usually share some knowledge of my cultural background with my students, and I encourage them to do the same. I have developed assignments that help me know my students as they learn to know one another while working individually and in groups. There are some assignments that encourage them to conduct in depth-research about other cultures in order to learn about their differences and their similarities. By the end of the semester, they usually become friends. They are still different but great friends with respect, tolerance, and admiration for one another.

Participant 6 helped her students understand and consider the importance of diversity. She developed class activities that raise openness, awareness, and tolerance for diversity. For instance, she worked with her students to give in-depth presentations about their countries and cultural background in order to educate their peers of their origins. She encouraged them to talk about some little-known fact about their countries and bring some valuable items from their countries to share with others.

Participant 7 integrated many multicultural activities in her classroom that emphasized acknowledging, accepting, tolerating, and transforming diversity into learning and living advantages.

Participant 8 suggested that multiculturalism played a major role in his curriculum. He explained:

> Each semester, most of my students are usually new to the United States. As I usually tell them, it is not enough for me to just teach them English. I have developed activities to help my students expand their skills and knowledge they need to succeed in the United States. I encourage them to acknowledge and value themselves and their classmates and develop behaviors that model the benefits of multiculturalism.

Participant 9 made extra effort to treat her students with the utmost respect. She said she had to pave the way with the idea that by showing the respect that her students deserved as humans, they would, in return, show respect to her, their classmates, and others. She suggested that the basic formula is showing respect, valuing others, and being polite toward others.

Participant 10 suggested that she mediated conversations by pointing out when others unconsciously stereotyped. She has carefully instructed them by using analogies to help them understand that anyone can be a victim of stereotyping. She encouraged her students to do the same.

As classrooms are becoming more culturally pluralistic and complex, the need to develop awareness and tolerance of diversity within those classrooms is pivotal. In Question 8, the researcher wanted to find the leadership mechanism that participants, as educators, employed to develop diversity awareness and tolerance in their classrooms. Participants noted it was a daunting task to make their classroom a culturally responsive environment for them and their students. They wanted their students to feel accepted and appreciated rather than ignored, feared, and judged. Participants claimed that they used a wide range of culturally responsive classroom activities that added value to the significance of students' cultural differences and demonstrated that each one of them mattered and was important, regardless of their ethnicities, their appearance, gender, age, and other diversity dimensions. Table 9 shows the emergent theme pertaining to the responses of participants to this question.

Table 9

Question 8 Emergent Theme

Theme	Responses of Participants
Integrating Diversity in Curriculum	Encouraging, inspiring, and developing tolerance for diversity in my classroom is a daily priority for me.
	Professors play a dominant role in helping their students valuing, accepting, and tolerating differences.
	I promote cultural harmony and acceptance by ensuring students are aware of stereotypes, generalizations, and culturally insensitivity when and if they ever use any in my presence.
	I always spend time creating an atmosphere where each student feels part of a friendly and safe learning environment.
	I have integrated diversity in my curricula.
	Understand and consider the importance of diversity.
	I have developed activities to help my students expand their skills and knowledge they need to succeed in the United States.

Question 9

How does your relationship with your leader (s) affect your contribution and commitment to your workplace?

Participant 1 shared the following to explain how his relationship with his leader affected his contribution and commitment to his workplace:

> My leader's behavior is exceptionally exemplary. I always want to be treated and be seen the way I see others. I feel that my leader has treated me with respect. She values me. She adds values to my ideas. She inspires me. She motivates me. I am happy. Her behaviors have greatly impacted my contribution and commitment to my work. It is significant for me to see and feel that I am valued, my contribution and my commitment are valued. Otherwise, I would not be around.

Participant 2 answered as follows: "I am fortunate to work in a workplace with a leader who encourages and supports her followers. She earns my loyalty or commitment to the institution."

Participant 4 was fully committed to her workplace. She stated: "I feel that my commitment has a lot to do with my good relationship with my leader. Considering the respect and appreciation she has shown, I hope I have contributed enough."

Participant 5 agreed that her leader's leadership practices defined her commitment and contribution to her workplace. She stated:

I feel that I know my leader and my leader knows me. My leader accepts me for me; she respects me; she has been very caring. She has encourages me to go beyond myself, and she has empowered me to develop myself. That is why I freely love to go beyond her expectations for the success of my department and my students.

Participant 6 felt supported by her leader. She explained that her leader demonstrated great emotional intelligence toward her subordinates. She admitted that her leader created a very supporting and caring working environment for everyone.

Participant 7's relationship with her leader defined her commitment, loyalty, and contribution to her workplace. She said that she felt supported by her leader, and her leader cared.

Participant 8 explained that his job was his passion. He would do it for free; however, he claimed that his relationship with his boss added to his passion and his love for the job. He stated:

She leads with great skills and her heart. In return, I always seek the best interest of the team. I have been blessed to work with my leader and my colleagues. She has created the best loving, caring, and supporting team. I will always feel happy to commit to my team.

Participant 9 referred to her leader as a very good role model. She claimed that her leader admired and supported individual initiatives. Furthermore, she admitted that her leader empowered her followers and treated them with the utmost respect. She added: "We do not really see each other that often; however, I know she is there and she cares." And participant 10 simply said: "Hugely. How my leader behaves has a direct effect on my motivation and desire to work here, contribute, and stay here."

As schools continue to expand into more complex learning and working environments, those changes raise significant leadership challenges. In a multicultural environment, through their behaviors, leaders play a major in balancing the needs of their institution with the personal and professional needs of their followers. In Question 9, the inquirer sought to investigate the leadership style of the leader and how it affected participants' contribution and commitment to their workplace. In both interviews, most participants praised the transformational leadership behaviors of their leader. Participants admitted their leader's cultural competency made diversity the fundamental sustainable resource of their department. As the environment keeps changing, their leader has continued to clearly communicate both short-term and long-term organizational vision and goals. Participants highlighted the following factors about their leader: (a) she listened, (b) she collaborated, (c) she cared, and (d) she empowered. Table 10 shows the emergent theme that developed from the question and participants' responses.

Table 10

Question 9 Emergent Theme

Theme	Reponses of Participants
Effective Multicultural Leadership	I feel that my leader values me. Her leadership behavior has greatly impacted my contribution and commitment to my work.
	She earns my loyalty or commitment to the institution.
	I feel that my commitment has a lot to do with my good relationship with my leader.
	She has encourages me to go beyond myself, and she has empowered me to develop myself.
	Leader has demonstrated great emotional intelligence towards her subordinates.
	Leader has created a very supporting and caring working environment for everyone.
	She leads with great skills and her heart.
	Leader admires and supports individual initiatives.
	How my leader behaves has a direct effect on my motivation and desire to work here, contribute, and stay here.

CHAPTER FIVE

DISCUSSION, CONCLUSIONS, RECOMMENDATIONS

In this qualitative phenomenological study, the researcher gained in-depth insight into the daily lived experiences of a diverse group of educators in their multicultural classroom and the leadership practices their leader used to develop a successful multicultural learning and working environment. A significant volume of literature and the findings from individual and group interviews were used as a basis of this study of participants' experiences with the phenomenon of the challenges and opportunities related to multiculturalism in the classrooms and effective multicultural leadership practices.

Summary of the Study

The analysis of the literature, the data collected from the interviews, and the reflective journal showed that: (a) the demographic changes in the U.S. population are being reflected on educational institutions, (b) the trends are real and significant, and (c) leaders of multicultural education institutions must take it upon themselves to match their leadership practices with the driving need to prioritize the benefits of diversity. The researcher conducted qualitative analysis to compare the themes from the literature review, the interviews, and the reflective journal and established triangulation to increase the validity and the credibility of the findings. The findings accurately reflected the daily lived experiences and the perceptions of the participants of diversity and their institution (Denzin & Lincoln, 2011; Merriam, 2009).

Participants discussed some common challenges they faced in performing their tasks as a team and in interacting with others (i.e., students and colleagues) from similar and different cultures. Shockley-Zalabak (2009) found that task, communication, and other cultural conflicts have significant bearings on team members' exchanges, relations, and organizational operations and outlets. Intrapersonal, interpersonal, small group, intergroup, and the environment can all be sources of organizational conflict. As most participants observed, in either situation, both team leaders and members need a good understanding of the roots and impacts of any particular conflict and must be able mobilize their efforts to develop a strategic plan to overcome obstacles (Garrison, Wakefield, Xu, & Kim, 2010; Marquardt, 2003; Shockley-Zalabak, 2009).

Participants explained the need to integrate multiculturalism in the curriculum, which has produced significant educational benefits for their students as suggested by Cheng et al. (2011). They discussed the complex and positive impact of this academic engagement. Some participants even agreed that the level of academic exposure to diversity in their classrooms helped increase the quality of the exchanges among students and their cognitive development, as supported by Nieto & Bode

(2012) and Olstad, Foster, & Wyman (1983). Participants suggested a more profound level of academic engagement of diversity for a greater spectrum of perspectives, opportunities, and academic success.

In order to multiply the benefits of multiculturalism on campuses, participants opined that leaders need to emphasize intercultural professional development for educators because they play the predominant role in leveraging diversity in their classrooms (Cheng et al., 2011; Nieto & Bode, 2012). Furthermore, some participants agreed that integrating diversity in the classroom does not simply come through hiring professionals of diverse background because diversity poses both social and pedagogical challenges. Educators must be prepared to ensure equitable opportunities for the personal and academic success of their students. Some acknowledged their lack of multicultural competence. Their lack of transcultural competence impacted their maturity and confidence in establishing exchanges with some of their students, understanding their behaviors, and responding effectively to their emotional and intellectual needs. As participants agreed, sustainable professional transcultural development is fundamental in integrating diversity in their classrooms (Cheng et al., 2011; Nieto & Bode, 2012; Olstad et al., 1983).

Summary of Study Purpose

The description of the experiences and perceptions of research participants was the focus of the study (Creswell, 2009). In using a transcendental research method and adopting the constructivist worldview, the researcher explored the phenomenon of the participants who led a successful teaching career in the face of substantial multicultural trends (Creswell, 2009; Moustakas, 1994). The main research question is: What are the lived experiences of a diverse group of educators in their multicultural classrooms and the leadership practices developed within their institution? The purpose of the study was to learn the views of the participants related to acknowledging, accepting, successfully managing multiculturalism, and multicultural leadership.

Research Design

The researcher used a qualitative research method to address the overarching research question for the study. Multiple unstructured individual interviews and one focus group interview were used to investigate the experiences and perceptions of a transcultural group of faculty members as to growing multiculturalism in the classroom and effective multicultural leadership. Based upon the literature of empirical researchers pertaining to diversity, multiculturalism, organizational conflicts, multicultural education, teaching in multicultural classrooms, integration of multiculturalism in the classroom, developing transformational and multicultural leadership, the researcher developed nine interview questions to study the daily lived experiences of the participants and leadership practices in their natural setting. Data pertaining to the ongoing phenomenon in the participants' working environment were collected beyond all prejudgments of the researcher, and qualitative analysis was conducted to look for emergent codes from the participants' responses.

Discussion of Results

An in-depth investigation of relevant literature revealed diversity has become a fact of the U.S. population and is having a lasting impact on educational institutions. The literature review highlighted controversial complexities and benefits in effectively integrating and managing diversity. All participants were deeply engaged and showed compelling interest in the research topic.

Ten participants were purposefully selected. All participated in the individual interview sessions, which were conducted before the group session. The inquirer purposely selected six of the participants for the focus group session because three voluntarily decided not to participate. The researcher chose not to invite the other participant because of her dominant leadership status in the institution. In both interview settings the researcher used the same predominant research questions to investigate the lived experiences of the participants and the leadership practices of their leader. Results from both phenomenological investigations were aligned with the literature review findings.

Ten themes that emerged of the literature review finding were similar to the findings of the study and formed the essence of the core interview questions. Themes were highlighted as follows: advantages of multiculturalism, disadvantages of multiculturalism, the importance of self-acknowledgement, cultural conflict, impact of culture on personal behavior, developing affirming diversity, accepting differences, need for professional multicultural education development, integrating diversity in curriculum, and effective multicultural leadership. The findings of the literature, the individual interviews, and the reflective journal were the basis of the focus group interview.

Major Research Findings

All participants agreed that multiculturalism can help staff, faculty, and students enrich their personal, educational, and professional experiences through interacting with others with different background, perspectives, beliefs, experiences, and nationalities. Findings from the study showed multiculturalism will continue to strengthen our classrooms as school leaders and faculty conscientiously emphasize its impact on the viability and vitality of the multicultural American society. As most participants suggested, multiculturalism does not cause any disadvantages; its trends highlight similarities, differences, understanding, and challenges, and foster significant impetus for necessary changes to develop inclusion, increase cognitive development, and facilitate professional and academic success (Achinstein & Athanases, 2005; Cheng et al., 2011).

Participants focused on the importance of developing affirming diversity, which emphasizes acknowledging and accepting differences. As suggested by Nieto and Bode (2012), affirming diversity offers conceptual and motivating tools for acceptance and integration and some degrees of freedom and security in expressing personal identities and being comfortable with differences. In developing affirming diversity, participants deepened their interests and matched them to the benefits of multiculturalism in order to ensure they created a diverse environment where all parties felt valued, respected, and accepted as valuable members of their classrooms and their institution (Goldsmith, Greenberg, Robertson, & Hu-Chan, 2003).

All participants agreed that a multicultural education program would be integral to improving their multicultural competence and preparing them for their pluralistic work environment (Shudak, 2010). Some participants explained how important it is to acknowledge, accept, and tolerate others and their differences and to acquire some basic education about different cultural dimensions and ethnically diverse people (Shudak, 2010).

The participants suggested effective multicultural leadership is an important goal for leaders to be consistently seeking in order to embrace diversity and ensure sustainable organizational success by genuinely managing to "maximize benefits and minimize negative consequences of workforce diversity" (Wolfson et al., 2011, p. 162; see also Madhlangobe & Gordon, 2012). Some participants agreed that employees need to assess, feel, and understand the need to deviate themselves from negative perceptions and prejudices, and personal beliefs for the greater good of the team, but first they have to know that their leaders have their best interests at heart (Dyer et al., 2007; Madhlangobe & Gordon, 2012; Maxwell, 1995). In private and in group, many participants praised their leader for her effective leadership practices and her understanding and support of their need to develop themselves and sustain resonating relationship across cultures. Participants were willing to develop the expertise expected of them to ensure the success of their students and their institution (Curry, Wergin, & Associates, 1993).

Study Implications

Two levels of focus for implications arose from the findings: (a) implications for educational institutions, and (b) implications for multicultural organizations. The findings of this study add to the increasing body of literature focused on the growing diversity of the U.S. population, how this diversity is reflected on our campuses, and the role of multicultural leaders in developing affirming diversity while capitalizing on differences. Findings suggest the impelling need for further study.

Implications for Educational Institution

The literature review for this research study showed that research in the area of multiculturalism in diverse institutions and multicultural leadership is an ongoing dilemma. Numerous findings from the existing literature demonstrated the imperative and compelling urgency for multiculturalism in our diverse classrooms because it is the right thing to do. The U.S. Supreme Court, in *Fisher v. University of Texas at Austin*, found multiculturalism to be one of the most dominant challenges and opportunities facing many education institutions, which they should openly and legally implement in their programs (U.S. Department of Education, 2013).

Hopefully, the findings of the current study and others will enable school leaders to value the benefits of multiculturalism and develop effective leadership practices that endorse multiculturalism. Diversity in schools emphasizes academic and social opportunities for students. In educational settings, it is pivotal that students feel culturally comfortable because culture can influence their level of academic commitment, comprehension, and achievement (Holmes et al., 1997; Triandis, 1995). Multiculturalism also shapes fundamental reputation and creates business opportunities and growth for higher institutions in their sternly competitive market (Holmes et al., 1997; Teixeira, Rocha, Biscaia, & Cardoso, 2012).

Implications for Organizations

Multiculturalism trends may impede national identity, organizational mission, vision, and core values, and foster multiple personal and task conflicts, yet have become a pivotal asset for human resources, innovation, larger market share and productivity, global competitive standing, and sustainable economic success (McKay et al., 2007). The findings of this study highlighted the increasing impetus for multicultural leaders to embrace, value, and capitalize on multiculturalism. Findings are clear on the fact that multiculturalism means adopting, beyond all geographical and other aspects of cultures, a universal culture to accept individuality, similarities, and differences to build a pluralistic inclusion and give everybody a face and a voice

(Arthur, Bell, Doverspike, & Villado, 2006; Bezrukova, Thatcher, & Jehn, 2007; Komives, 2010; McCulloch & Turban, 2007). Leaders should not remain idle while diversity is becoming a global fact of life (Berman & Victorian Equal Opportunity and Human Rights Commission, 2008; Elems, 2011; Komives, 2010). Leaders are to be at the forefront in building inclusion in accepting everybody with their unique differences, their unique faces, and their unique voices because diversity is the magnet that attracts all differences (Arthur et al., 2006; Bezrukova et al., 2007; Green, 2010; Komives, 2010; McKay et al., 2007; U.S. Office of Personnel Management, 2000).

Recommendations for Future Research

Multiculturalism defines the existence of the complex American society, as it promotes educational, personal, and professional growth in an increasingly pluralistic society. As multiculturalism continues to affect the competitive American standing in the global market, its private and public institutions, and its families, school leaders will need to keep developing and improving their indubitable role in developing, sustaining, and making effective use of diversity. The findings of this research study and relevant literature review illustrated the following considerable recommendations that can be relevant to future researchers:

- The researcher did not ask participants to discuss whether they knew that their current workplace was so diverse before they joined it. A more in-depth study may need to address that question. Most participants claimed they did not have enough preparation in terms of multicultural competency. Responses showed many participants did not know much about the culture of their institution; some of them even showed some remorse for their lack of preparation, which could have affected their decision to join their institution had they been aware of the environment.

- The study only reflected the experiences of the participants in their current workplace, which may have limited participants' responses in the study. Other researchers could go further in developing questions that go beyond participants' experiences in their work environment. It is the inquirer's assumption that answers could be different because participants would have more to share. Previous experiences in other work environments and general exposure to multiculturalism in their personal lives may affect their assumptions, behaviors, and expectations when interacting with their diverse co-workers and students. It is also worth noting that the participants' workplace has developed a very active diversity department, which could have influenced participants' perceptions of their workplace and their responses.

- The study built the case for multiculturalism in diverse classrooms and multicultural leadership which reflected the research question and the interview questions. The literature review showed a significant lack of empirical study on whether multiculturalism would benefit all parties. One study showed diversity does not have any long-term positive impact on students (Arcidiacono & Vigdor, 2010).

- The study suggested the need for multicultural education development; however, there was no question about how much of it was needed or any specific role that participants would want it to play in the process. Would that program be mandatory or optional? All participants agreed there was a need for a multicultural education development program, but not everyone has the same needs or the same level of multicultural competency. Some participants mentioned that they were making baby steps accepting differences. Others had no previous experience working or living in a diverse work environment.

- One additional factor that was not discussed in the study that may offer more insight is to use a larger sample, more than one institution, and other forms of data collection instruments. Those components would enable more data collection, which could help develop a better picture of the phenomenon.

Generalizability and Limitations

Generalizability is significant in establishing research credibility. The researcher developed a literature review map and followed Lincoln and Guba's (2000) recommendations pertaining to "credibility, transferability, dependability, and confirmability" (Schwandt, 2007, p. 18) of qualitative research, as discussed in Chapter 3 of this study. However, some issues bring into question the generalizability of the study.

The inquirer sought to investigate the daily lived experiences of a group of college professors from different cultural background and nationalities in their multicultural classrooms and leadership practices within their institution. At the time of the study, they were working at a highly diverse educational institution. The phenomenon was that the growing diversity of the U.S. population is being played out on their campus and in their classrooms. Every day they faced the compelling challenges of multiculturalism while interacting with co-workers and developing an effective learning environment for their diverse students.

The researcher conducted a phenomenological study using open-ended questions in unstructured interviews to better understand an ongoing issue (Creswell, 2009). Research participants were purposefully selected educators who had extended experience working in other previous multicultural environments, and they had been working together for more than 5 years in their current institution. Some of the participants had been in leadership positions. Thus, the researcher used expert sampling because participants were experienced and knowledgeable of the research topic and their field, and their responses pertained to the literature review findings (Creswell, 2009; Moustakas, 1994).

Each participant was unique and had his or her own views on the research topic, and the interview questions, perceptions of culture and multiculturalism, personal and professional experiences living and working in a homogenous or a diverse environment. Also, the institution (research site) was unique with its phenomenon, its leaders and members, and its multicultural policies.

Other factors affected the generalizability of the findings. For instance, the overreaching research question and the core interview questions were objectively written and addressed to enable the collection of open and unbiased qualitative data. Other questions were addressed to keep the conversations emerging. Participants were allowed to share their stories, their feelings, and their perceptions. Validating qualitative data were collected in implementing triangulation of data.

This study involved an investigation of the phenomenon of a specific group of participants in their natural setting. Rigorous efforts were developed to ensure credibility, dependability, transferability, and confirmability. Findings were aligned with findings from other studies. The study was beneficial to the literature as its findings highlighted the need for further research; nonetheless, the results cannot be generalized in other educational institutions (De Vaus, 2005).

Conclusion

This phenomenological study included a review of pertinent literature pertaining to the growing trend of multiculturalism in schools across the United States of America. Relevant literature was reviewed to investigate the impelling need for and the richness of diversity. An analysis of the qualitative data collected was conducted to investigate the daily lived experiences and the cultural perceptions of ten English as Second Language professors in their cross-cultural natural setting in the leadership practices within their institution.

As a result of this study, it can be concluded that there is an increasing focus on multiculturalism, its trends, its intricacies, and its benefits in integrating it into the classrooms. Furthermore, the study extended past research and likewise accentuated the academic, personal, professional, and social, benefits of multiculturalism education, as long as school leaders value the means to acknowledge, integrate, and align it with the goals, the resources, the practices, and the values of their institutions (DeSimone & Werner, 2012; Mello, 2011).

REFERENCES

Achinstein, B., & Athanases, S. Z. (2005). Focusing new teachers on diversity and equity: Toward a knowledge base for mentors. *Teaching and Teacher Education, 21*, 843-862.

Adam, M. (2010). A shifting diversity: Implications of legal changes in diversity in higher education. *The Hispanic Outlook in Higher Education, 21*(6), 14-16.

Alston-Mills, B. (2011). Using appreciative inquiry to promote diversity in higher education. *Journal of Diversity Management, 6*(3), 1.

Antelo, A., Prilipko, E., & Sheridan-Pereira, M. (2010). Assessing effective attributes of followers in a leadership process. *Contemporary Issues in Education Research, 3*(10), 1-12.

Arcidiacono, P., & Vigdor, J. L. (2010). Does the river spill over? Estimating the economic returns to attending a racially diverse college. *Economic Inquiry, 48*(3), 537-557.

Arthur, W., Jr., Bell, S. T., Doverspike, D., & Villado, A. J. (2006). The use of person-organization fit in employment decision-making: An assessment of its criterion-

related validity. *Journal of Applied Psychology,*
91(4), 786-801.

Barbuto, J. E., Jr. (2005). Motivation and
transactional, characteristic, and
transformational leadership: A test of
antecedents. *Journal of Leadership and*
Organizational Studies, 11(4), 26-40.

Barbuto, J. E., Jr., & Burback, M. E. (2006). The
emotional intelligence of transformational
leaders: A field study of elected officials.
The Journal of Social Psychology, 146(1), 51-64.

Barmaki, R. (2008). The relationship between
justice and freedom in Emile Durkheim's
thought. *International Journal of Criminology*
and Sociological Theory, 1(1), 51-61.

Barnhardt, C. L. (2014). Occupying the academy:
Just how important is diversity work in
higher education? *Journal of College Student*
Development, 55(2), 218-220.

Bennis, W. (1994). *On becoming a leader.*
Wilmington, MA: Warren Bennis.

Berman, G., & Victorian Equal Opportunity and Human Rights Commission. (2008). *Harnessing diversity: Addressing racial and religious discrimination in employment.* Melbourne: Victorian Multicultural Commission and the Victorian Equal Opportunity & Human Rights Commission.

Bernard, H. R., & Ryan, G. W. (2010). *Analyzing qualitative data: System approaches.* Thousand Oaks, CA: Sage.

Bezrukova, K., Thatcher, S. M. B., & Jehn, K. (2007). Group heterogeneity and faultiness: Comparing alignment and dispersion theories of group composition. In K. J. Behfar, & L. L. Thompson (Eds.), *Conflict in organizational groups: New directions in theory and practice* (pp. 57-92). Evanston, IL: The Northwestern University Press.

Branch, A. (2001). Retaining African-Americans in higher education. In L. Jones (Ed.), *How to retain African-American faculty during times of challenge for higher education* (pp. 175-191). Sterling, VA: Stylus Publishing.

Burdett, J., & Crossman, J. (2012). Engaging international students: An analysis of the Australian Universities Quality Agency

(AUQA) reports. *Quality Assurance in Education, 20*(3), 207-222.

Canfield-Davis, K., Tenuto, P., Jain, S., & McMurtry, J. (2011). Professional ethical obligations for multicultural education and implications for educators. *Academy of Educational Leadership Journal, 15*(1), 95-116.

Capell, J., Dean, E., & Veenstra, G. (2008). The relationship between cultural competence and ethnocentrism of healthcare professionals. *Journal of Transcultural Nursing, 19*(2), 121-124.

Castaneda, M. E., & Bateh, J. (2013). Strategies for multicultural management: Communication and a common set of values. *Journal of International Education Research, 9*(1), 41.

Chatman, J., & Cha, S. (2003). Leading by leveraging culture. *California Management Review, 45*(4), 20-34.

Chen, Y., Wang, W. C., & Chu, Y. C. (2011). Infiltration of the multicultural awareness: Multinational enterprise strategy management. *International Journal of Business and Management, 6*(2), 72-76.

Cheng, L., Wang, Z., & Zhang, W. (2011). The effects of conflict on team decision making. *Social Behavior and Personality, 39*(2), 189-198.

Clark, C. (2011). Diversity initiatives in higher education: Just how important is diversity in higher education? *Multicultural Education, 18*(3), 57-59.

Clegg, S., Kornberger, M., & Rhodes, C. (2007). Organizational ethics, decision making undecidability. *The Editorial Board of the Sociological Review, 55*(2), 393-409.

Creswell, J. W. (2009). *Research design: Qualitative, quantitative, and mixed methods approaches* (3rd ed.). Thousand Oaks, CA: Sage Publications.

Curry, L., Wergin, J. F., & Associates. (1993). *Educating professionals: Responding to new expectations for competence and accountability.* San Francisco, CA: Jossey-Bass.

Daft, R. L. (2008). *The leadership experience* (4th ed.). Mason, OH: South-Western Cengage Learning.

DeMarrais, K. (2004). *Qualitative interview studies: Learning through experience.* Mahwah, NJ: Erlbaum.

De Vaus, D. A. (2005). *Research design in social research.* Thousand Oaks, CA: Sage.

Denzin, N. K., & Lincoln, Y. S. (2011). *The Sage handbook of qualitative research* (4th ed.). Thousand Oaks, CA: Sage.

DeSimone, R. L., & Werner, J. M. (2012). *Human resource development* (6th ed.). Canada: Cengage Learning.

Doyle, R., & George, U. (2008). Achieving and measuring diversity: An organizational change approach. *Social Work Education, 27*(1), 97-110.

Dudas, K. I. (2012). Cultural competence: An evolutionary concept analysis. *Nursing Education Perspectives, 33*(5), 317-321.

Dyer, W., Dyer, G., & Dyer, J. (2007). *Team building: Proven strategies for improving team performance* (4th ed.). San Francisco, CA: Jossey-Bass.

Elems, U. (2011). Leading with cultural intelligence: The new secret to success. *The Journal of Applied Christian Leadership, 5*(1), 102-104.

Ford, D. Y. (2005). Welcoming all students to room 202: Creating culturally responsive classrooms. *Gifted Child Today, 28*(4), 28-30, 65.

Garrison, G., Wakefiled, R., Xu, X., & Kim, S. (2010). Globally distributed teams: The effect of diversity on trust, cohesion and individual performance. *The Data Base for Advances in Information Systems, 41*(3), 27-48.

Giger, J., Davidhizar, R., Purnell, L., Harden, J., Phillips, J., & Strickland, O. (2007). American Academy of Nursing Expert Panel Report: Developing cultural competence to eliminate health disparities in ethnic minorities and other vulnerable populations. *Journal of Transcultural Nursing, 18*, 95-102.

Gilgun, J. F. (2010). Reflexivity and qualitative research. *Current Issues in Qualitative Research, 1*(2), 1-8.

Gill, A., Fitzgerald, S., Bhutani, S., Mand, H., & Sharma, S. (2010). The relationship between transformational leadership and employee desire for empowerment. *International Journal of Contemporary Hospital Management, 22*(2), 263-273.

Goldsmith, M., Greenberg, C., Robertson, A., & Hu-Chan, M. (2003). *Global leadership: The next generation for Education Management Corporation.* Upper Saddle River, NJ: Pearson Learning Solutions.

Grambrill, E. (2006). *Social work practice: A critical thinker's guide* (2nd ed.). New York, NY: Oxford University Press.

Green, T. K. (2010). Race and sex in organizing work: "Diversity", discrimination and integration. *Emory Law Journal, 59*(3), 585-647.

Guerra, P. L., & Nelson, S. W. (2007). Cultural proficiency: The journey to cultural proficiency is a sizeable challenge. *JSD (National Staff Development Council), 28*(4), 59-60.

Hansuvadha, N., & Slater, C. L. (2012). Culturally competent school leaders: The individual and the system. *The Education Forum, 76*, 174-189.

Hennink, M., Hutter, I., & Bailey, A. (2011). *Qualitative research methods*. Thousand Oaks, CA: Sage.

Hofstede, G. (1991) *Culture and organizations: Software of the mind.* New York, NY: McGraw-Hill.

Holmes, G., Sherman, T., & Williams-Green, J. (1997). Culture as a decision variable for designing computer software. *Educational Technology Systems, 26*(1), 3-18.

Igwebuike, J. G. (2006). Legal and policy implications for faculty diversification in higher education. *Negro Educational Review, 57*(3/4), 189.

Jackson, S. E., May, K. E., & Whitney, K. (1995). Understanding the dynamics of diversity in decision-making teams. In R. A. Guzzo, E. Salas, & Associates (Eds.), *Team effectiveness and decision making in organizations* (pp. 204-261). San Francisco, CA: Jossey-Bass.

Jacobs, L. C., & Friedman, C. B. (1988). Student achievement under foreign teaching associates compared with native teaching associates. *The Journal of Higher Education, 59*(5), 551-563.

Joplin, J. R. W., & Daus, C. S. (1997). Challenges of leading a diverse workforce. *The Academy of Management Perspectives, 11*(3), 32-47.

Kankanhalli, A., Tan, B. C. Y., & Wei, K. (2006). Conflict and performance in global virtual teams. *Journal of Management Information Systems, 23*(3), 237-274.

Keung, E., & Rockinson-Szapkiw, A. (2013). The relationship between transformational leadership and cultural intelligence: A study of international school leaders. *Journal of Educational Administration, 51*(6), 836-854.

Kidder, M. R. (1995). *How good people make tough choices: Resolving the dilemmas of ethical living.* New York, NY: Harper Collins.

Kitagawa, F., & Oba, J. (2010). Managing differentiation of higher education system in Japan: Connecting excellence and diversity. *Higher Education, 59*(4), 507-524.

Klein, H. J. (1989). An integrated control theory model of work motivation. *Academy of Management Review, 14*(2), 150-172.

Komives, S. R. (2010). Rethinking leadership practices in a complex, multicultural, and global environment: New concepts and models for higher education. *Review of Higher Education, 34*(1), 186-188.

Kouzes, M. J., & Posner, B. Z. (2008). *The student leadership challenge.* San Francisco, CA: John Wiley & Sons.

Kumar, R. (2011). *Research methodology* (3rd ed.). Thousand Oaks, CA: Sage Publications.

Ladson-Billings, G. (2002). *Crossing over to Canaan: The journey of new teachers in diverse classrooms.* San Francisco, CA: Jossey-Bass.

Ladson-Billings, G. (2009). *The dreamkeepers; Successful teachers of African American children* (2nd ed.). San Francisco, CA: Jossey-Bass.

Lauring, J., & Selmer, J. (2012). Openness to diversity, trust, and conflict in multicultural organizations. *Journal of Management & Organization, 18*(6), 795-806.

Lee, G., & Janda, L. (2005). *College students' perceptions of faculty's teaching ability based on their ethnicity, accent, and academic discipline.* Unpublished manuscript.

Lee, H. E., Park, H. S., Lee, T. A., & Lee, D. W. (2007). Relationships between LMX and subordinates' feedback-seeking. *Social Behavior & Personality: An International Journal, 35*(5), 659-674.

Lincoln, Y. S., & Guba, E. G. (2000). Paradigmatic controversies, contradictions, and emerging influences. In N. K. Lincoln (Eds.), *The Sage handbook of qualitative research* (3rd ed., pp. 191-215). Thousand Oaks, CA: Sage.

Liu, B., Liu, J., & Hu, J. (2010). Person-organization fit, job satisfaction, and turnover intention: An empirical study in the Chinese public sector. *Social Behavior and Personality, 38*(5), 615-626.

Liua, C., Nautab, M. N., Spectorc, P. E., & Lid, C. (2008). Direct and indirect conflicts at work in China and the US: A cross-cultural comparison. *Work & Stress, 22*(4), 295-313.

Locke, L. F., Silverman, S. J., & Spriduso, W. W. (2010). *Reading and understanding research* (3rd ed.). Thousand Oaks, CA: Sage Publications.

Lunenburg, F. C. (2010). Leader-member exchange theory: Another perspective on the leadership process. *International Journal of Management, Business, and Administration, 13*(1), 1-5.

Madhlangobe, L., & Gordon, S. P. (2012). Culturally responsive leadership in a diverse school: A case study of a high school leader. *NASSP Bulletin, 96*(3), 177-202.

Maharaj, R. (2007). Corporate governance, groupthink and bullies in the boardroom. *International Journal of Disclosure and Governance, 5*(1), 69-92.

Marquardt, M. J. (2003). Developing global leaders via action learning programs: A case study at Boeing. *Thai Journal of Public Administration, 3*(3), 133-157.

Marsella, A. J. (2009). Diversity in a global era: The context and consequences of differences. *Counselling Psychology Quarterly, 22*(1), 119-135.

Maxwell, J. C. (1995). *Developing the leaders around you.* Nashville, TN: Thomas Nelson.

Mayer, J. D., Salovey, P., & Caruso, D. R. (2004). Emotional intelligence: Theory, findings, and implications. *Psychological Inquiry, 15*(3), 197-215.

McCoy, B. H. (2007). *Living into leadership: A journey in ethics.* Stanford, CA: Stanford University Press.

McCulloch, M. C., & Turban, D. B. (2007). Using person-organization fit to select employees for high turnover jobs. *International Journal of Selection and Assessment, 15*(1), 63-71.

McKay, P. F., Avery, D. R., Tonidandel, S., Morris, M. A., Hernandez, M., & Hebl, M. R. (2007). Racial differences in employee retention: Are diversity climate perceptions the key? *Personnel Psychology, 60*(1), 35-62.

Mello, J. A. (2011). *Strategic management of human resources* (3rd ed.). Canada: Cengage Learning.

Merriam, S. B. (1998). *Qualitative research and case study applications in education*. San Francisco, CA: Jossey-Bass.

Merriam, S. B. (2009). *Qualitative research: A guide to design and implementation*. San Francisco, CA: Jossey-Bass.

Moustakas, C. (1994). *Phenomenological research methods*. Thousand Oaks, CA: Sage Publications.

Murdock, S. (2006). *Population change in the United States: Implications for human and socioeconomic resources in the 21st century*. San Antonio, TX: Institute for Demographic and Socioeconomic Research, University of Texas San Antonio.

Nieto, S., & Bode, P. (2012). *Affirming diversity the sociopolitical context of multicultural education* (6th ed.). Boston, MA: Pearson Education.

Northouse, P. G. (2001). *Leadership theory and practice* (2nd ed.). Thousand Oaks, CA: Sage Publications.

Olstad, R. G., Foster, C. D., & Wyman, R. M. (1983). Multicultural education for preservice teachers. *Integrated Education, 21*, 137-139.

Orwin, C. (1996). All quiet on the post(western) front? *Public Interest, 123*, 3-21.

Ostergaard, C., Timmermans, B., & Kristinsson, K. (2011). Does a different view create something new? The effect of employee diversity on innovation. *Research Policy, 40*(3), 500-509.

Patton, M. Q. (2002). *Qualitative research and evaluation methods* (3rd ed.). Thousand Oaks, CA: Sage Publications.

Pedersen, P. B., & Connerly, M. L. (2005). *Leadership in a diverse and multicultural environment.* Thousand Oaks, CA: Sage Publications.

Pedersen, P. B., Draguns, J. G., Lonner, W. J., & Trimble, J. E. (2008). *Counseling across cultures* (6th ed.). Thousand Oaks, CA: Sage Publications.

Perkins, D. N. T., Holtman, M. P., Kessler, P. R., & McCarthy, C. (1942). *Leading at the edge.* New York, NY: American Management Association.

Pew Research Center. (2014). *America's racial tapestry is changing.* Retrieved from http://www.pewresearch.org./next-america/#Americas-Racial-Tapestry-Is-Changing

Prilipko, E. V., Antelo, A., & Henderson, R. L. (2011). Rainbow of followers' attributes in a leadership process. *International Journal of Management and Information Systems, 15*(2), 74-94.

Purnell, L. (2005). The Purnell model for cultural competence. *Journal of Multicultural Nursing & Health, 11*(2), 7-15.

Rahim, M. A. (2011). *Managing conflict in organizations* (4th ed.). New Brunswick, NJ: Transactions.

Razak, N. A., Darmawan, G. N., & Keeves, J. P. (2010). The influence of culture on teacher commitment. *Social Psychology of Education, 13*(2), 185-205.

Rice, M. F. (2005). *Diversity and public administration.* Armonk, NY: M. E. Sharpe.

Roper, L. D. (2011). Supervising across cultures: Navigating diversity and multiculturalism. *New Directions for Students Services, 136*, 69-80.

Savory, A., & Butterfield, J. (1999). *Holistic management: A new framework for decision making.* Washington, DC: Island Press.

Schaubroeck, J., Lam, S. S. K., & Cha, S. E. (2007). Embracing transformational leadership: Team values and the impact of leader behavior on team performance. *Journal of Applied Psychology, 92*(4), 1020-1030.

Schim, S., Doorenbos, A., & Borse, N. (2006). Enhancing cultural competence among hospice staff. *American Journal of Hospice and Palliative Medicine, 23*, 404-411.

Schwandt, T. A. (2007). *Dictionary of qualitative inquiry* (3rd ed.). Thousand Oaks: CA: Sage.

Shockley-Zalabak, P. S. (2009). *Fundamentals of organization communication* (7th ed.). Boston, MA: Pearson Education.

Shudak, N. J. (2010). Diversity in teacher education: A double helix. *Academic Questions, 23*(3), 348-355.

Smith, S. V. (2006). Encouraging the use of reflexivity in the writing up of qualitative research. *International Journal of Therapy and Rehabilitation, 13*(5), 209-215.

Stahl, G. K., Maznevski, M. L., Voigt, A., & Jonsen, K. (2010). Unraveling the effects of cultural diversity in teams: A meta-analysis of research on multicultural work groups. *Journal of international Business Studies, 41*, 690-709.

Strauss, A. L. (1987). *Qualitative analysis for social scientists*. New York, NY: Cambridge University Press.

Teixeira, P. N., Rocha, V., Biscaia, R., & Cardoso, M. F. (2012). Competition and diversity in higher education: An empirical approach to specialization patterns of Portuguese institutions. *Higher Education, 63*(3), 337-352.

Triandis, H. C. (1995). *Individualism and collectivism*. Boulder, CO: Westview Press.

Triandis, H. C. (2001). Individualism-collectivism and personality. *Journal of Personality, 69*(6), 909-912.

U.S. Census Bureau. (2008). *State and county quickfacts*. Retrieved from http://quickfacts.census.gov/qfd.states/00000.html

U.S. Department of Education. (2013). *New guidance supports voluntary use of race to achieve diversity in higher education*. Retrieved from http://www.ed.gov/news/press-releases/new-guidance-supports-voluntary-use-race-achieve-diversity-higher-education

U.S. Office of Personnel Management. (2000). *Building and maintaining a diverse and high quality workforce: A guide for federal agencies.* Washington, DC: Author.

Visagie, J., Linde, H., & Havenga, W. (2011). Leadership competencies for managing diversity. *Managing Global Transition, 9*(3), 225-247.

Watt, D. (2007). On becoming a qualitative researcher: The value of reflexivity. *The Qualitative Report, 12*(1), 82-101.

Webb, K. (2007). Motivating peak performance: Leadership behaviors that stimulate employee motivation and performance. *Christian Higher Education, 6*, 53-71.

Wiersma, W. (2000). *Research methods in education: An introduction.* Boston, MA: Allyn and Bacon.

Wolfson, N., Kraiger, K., & Finkelstein, L. (2011). The relationship between diversity climate perceptions and workplace attitudes. *The Psychologist-Manager Journal, 14*(3), 161-176.

Yukl, G. (1998). *Leadership in organizations* (4th ed.). South Brunswick, NJ: Harper Collins.

Zaccaro, S., Rittman, A., & Marks, M. (2001). Team leadership. *Leadership Quarterly, 12(*4), 451-483.

About the Author

Dr. Arthur Boyer is a native of Port-au-Prince, Haiti. He immigrated to the United States, in 1991. Dr. Boyer received his Bachelor of Science Degree in Criminal Justice, his Master's Degree in Public Administration from Hodges University, and his Doctorate Degree in Organizational Leadership from Argosy University.

Dr. Boyer is the Director of Academic Affairs and a lecturer at Southwestern Vocational Training, and an English professor at Hodges University. His distinguished leadership and teaching philosophy emphasize: transforming and sharing knowledge, facilitating understanding, theory and application, challenging and encouraging critical thinking, and creative experimentation.

Dr. Boyer is also an organizational leadership and academic coach, a motivational speaker, a radio commentator, and a columnist who has published and presented extensively. The essence of his writings and speeches entail: education, community leadership, civic engagement, multiculturalism's intricacies and benefits in integrating and aligning it with organizational goals, resources, the practices, and the core values of multicultural environments. Dr. Boyer believes that diversity is the magnet that attracts all differences.